# Untangling the Sexual Revolution

## Other Books on Contemporary Issues

# Untangling the Sexual Revolution

## Rethinking Our Sexual Ethic

by

Henry W. Spaulding II, Ph.D.

Beacon Hill Press of Kansas City
Kansas City, Missouri

ISBN: 083-411-3058

Printed in the
United States of America


Cover Design: Paul Franitza



Unless otherwise indicated, all scriptures are from *The Holy Bible, New International Version* (NIV), copyright © 1973, 1978, 1984 by the International Bible Society, and are used by permission.

Permission to quote from the following copyrighted version is acknowledged with appreciation:

The *New American Standard Bible* (NASB), © The Lockman Foundation, 1960, 1962, 1963, 1968, 1971, 1972, 1973, 1975, 1977.

King James Version (KJV).


10   9   8   7   6   5   4   3   2   1

To

Sharon Walker Spaulding

wife, lover, friend, mother,
theological critic, fellow pilgrim

# Contents

# Preface

Why another book on sexual ethics? This question occurred to me long before the first word was written in this book. Every Christian publisher has some volume to display in the area of sexual ethics. Some of these books are insightful, and it would seem that most of the issues have been raised. I write for two reasons. First, it seems that society is raising afresh the issue of human sexuality. All over the evangelical church questions concerning premarital sex, homosexuality, and the like are being asked with new intensity. Second, because of our society's mind-set a new approach is warranted. Every conceivable argument against sexual immorality has already been advanced. Therefore, we need to take a step back and ask about the theological foundations of morality. For these two reasons it seems a new volume might be needed and useful.

A word about my method might enhance the understanding of this volume. My particular training and interest lie in the area of theology and ethics. Through the many years of academic work, pastoring, and teaching it has become evident that in the Christian context theology and ethics are interdependent. When ethics are detached from theology, significant problems result. At one level this book is an argument for creatively joining theology and ethics. Moral responsibility is most clearly understood in light of its theological foundations. Therefore, we treat self-respect as a moral concept by calling attention to the doctrine of creation. We add to this the treatment of the Pauline teaching concerning the temple of the Holy Spirit and the Resurrection. It is my deep conviction that a full understanding of our theological resources will illuminate our moral responsibilities.

Theology is more than the treatment of scriptural truth and its theological interpretation. In order for theology to have an impact, it must be able and willing to confront the social sciences. Psychology and sociology are particularly relevant, but other disciplines are important as well. Theology can become enclosed in its own little box (the famous "ivory tower"); and when this happens, it loses its power to communicate. My vision for theology is that it move to another stage and engage life with all of its dynamism. I trust that some of that spirit is evident in the pages that follow.

The plan of this book is straightforward. Chapter 1 is a theological analysis of contemporary American life. It will illuminate some of the major moral issues we face. Chapters 2, 3, and 4 attempt to develop three biblically grounded and theologically balanced principles for untangling the sexual revolution. A particular pattern is used in each of these chapters. The beginning portion of each chapter sets forth the theological resources available. The conclusion of each of these chapters calls special attention to moral issues. Resist the temptation to read each part separately. If you read the theological before reading the ethical section, the argument will make more sense. A fifth chapter addresses the phenomenon of homosexuality and presents a perspective for the ministry of the Church. The final chapter attempts to pull everything together. The four lessons shared in this chapter in some measure crystallize the content of the previous chapters.

Writing this book has been difficult yet satisfying. The research and the writing have allowed me to formulate a clearer understanding of the gospel call to holiness/wholeness. Our generation is asking questions. They will find them answered in either secularism or the Christian gospel. It is my firm hope that our young will find the answer to life's deepest questions in the gospel. To this end I offer these pages.

Untangling the Sexual Revolution

# 1

# The End Is Now the Beginning

As the smoke begins to clear from the turbulence of the sexual revolution, a significantly changed landscape is emerging. The 1960s began with "Leave It to Beaver," but the 1980s inherited "Three's Company." Now that the revolution seems to have ended, some are tempted to relax, but such an attitude is premature. According to one prominent evangelical theologian, "There is no going back to the innocence of the 1950s."[1] We must walk boldly into the next century with a gospel that is both biblically grounded and courageously contemporary.

Several years ago I was on my way to a ministers' conference in Maine. As I was driving through Portland, a pickup truck passed me on the highway. It was dirty and dilapidated, but a bumper sticker on the back window was plainly visible. It read, "Question Authority." This little slogan might as well be etched on the forehead of a large number of people in America who say, in so many words, "Don't tell me what to do!" "I'm going to have it my way!" "If it feels good, do it!" This attitude has political overtones, but at an even more profound level its significance is moral. The gospel is in every way opposed to this kind of attitude.

The purpose of this book is to examine the sexual revolution as one manifestation of this broader cultural mood. The rejection of all authority quickly leads to moral license. Yesterday's news has become today's accepted behavior. Yet at an even deeper level the sexual revolution has affected every person. For the most part, the long hair and the anti-establishment slogans have vanished. But the changes wrought by all of this have left deep impressions upon our society and our faith. According to James Nelson, "The Sexual Revolution of the '60s and '70s is mostly over, and some of its superficial and exploitative forms have proven to be just that. Hurt, boredom, and disease have sobered more than a few—and the forces of religious and political reaction rejoice."[2] Nelson believes that the real revolution is only beginning. What may appear to some as an end is actually a call to action. We must look to this new world with a commitment grounded in the gospel but with our eyes wide open.

The following pages will analyze the deeper meaning of the sexual revolution. First, we'll define in basic terms the events usually associated with the sexual revolution. Then we will examine the major cultural milestones of our century. The premise here is that all revolutions begin in the realm of ideas. It should become clear that the self-assured slumber of some Christians is ill-advised.

## The Sexual Revolution: A Preliminary Analysis

**Historical Description.** Simply put, the sexual revolution refers to the period in American society that led to a more open and informed discussion of human sexuality. Certain excesses accompanied this revolution: Premarital intercourse, the open marriage, homosexuality, and other such expressions of sexuality came out of the closet between 1960 and 1971. But there was a positive side to the revolution as well. It led many to embrace a more healthy view of sexuality. This tension between the exploitative and the appropriate expression of sexuality makes sweeping generalizations about the sexual revolution unwise.

It is necessary to examine the 1960s for a clear understanding of the sexual revolution. Leonard Sweet divides the 1960s into the first '60s (1960-67) and the second '60s (1967-71). The first period he characterizes by the civil rights movement, situation ethics, and radical theology. This period is represented by people like Martin Luther King, Jr.,

Joseph Fletcher, and Thomas Altizer. During this period humanity celebrated its newfound identity; it was a time of hope and possibility. The second '60s stand in stark contrast to this hope. Here words like *hysteria, panic, chaos,* and *disintegration* are more typical.[3] The decade that had witnessed the moving speeches of John F. Kennedy and Martin Luther King, Jr., had also witnessed the brutal slaying of both men. The morality that had celebrated its autonomy in the first '60s was hopelessly lost in ambiguity and meaninglessness in the second '60s.

The historical and cultural forces that resulted in the sexual revolution go back much farther than the '60s. In fact, they reach all the way back into the previous century. Names like Friedrich Nietzsche, Sigmund Freud, and Charles Darwin figure very importantly in the undercurrents that eventually were manifested in the sexual revolution. We will examine more fully these cultural dispositions in the next section. According to Allan Bloom, a professor of philosophy at the University of Chicago:

> Sexual liberation presented itself as a bold affirmation of the senses and of undeniable natural impulse against our puritanical heritage, society's conventions and repressions, bolstered by Biblical myths about original sin. From the early sixties on there was a gradual testing of the limits on sexual expression, and they melted away or had already disappeared without anybody's having noticed it.[4]

Specifically, the sexual revolution represents a shift from a negative to a positive attitude toward sex. Before the revolution any serious discussion of sex was suppressed; afterward sex became the object of serious questions. There was also a shift away from strict control of sexual expression to a more tolerant attitude.[5] What followed these shifts are the more recognized excesses associated with the sexual revolution.

**The Meaning of the Sexual Revolution.** Society has changed forever because of the sexual revolution. The most obvious change relates to views on sexuality. What could be mentioned only in the most private of situations is now prime-time programming. My mother, who is a schoolteacher, recently found two five-year-old children attempting to have sexual intercourse during recess. The images that pervade our culture are so deeply sexual that they seem to be a national obsession. Nudity in the movie industry is commonly accepted. Pornography is available to almost anyone who has the money. Until very recently children could access "Dial-a-Porn" numbers and hear things that once would have shocked adults. Sexuality is considered by many to be a consumable product.

The separation of sexual behavior from the rest of life lies at the heart of the sexual revolution. We need to reintroduce the question of morality into American life. All too often we clamor after the flashy and the famous. These are not evil in and of themselves, but are our heroes interested in morality? Are we interested in the way people conduct themselves? Is it important that our heroes have moral qualities? For some the sexual revolution means that morality has nothing to do with sexuality.

What all of this means is that strange new pressures are placed on the young. About 10 years ago an anthropologist announced that virginity was a thing of the past for most adolescents. It is difficult to avoid the conclusion of one theologian: "Young people today are socially pressured to be sexually active long before they have been prepared educationally and psychologically to cope with the deeply personal and highly charged nature of sexuality."[6]

A pastor told me he attempted to address some of these pressures with his teens and met extreme opposition from the parents:

"Our children don't need this!"

"The church has no role in the education of our children in these matters!"

The opposition was so enormous that the pastor finally relented and canceled the class. Two years later four of the teens in the class were pregnant and had to marry quickly. Three of those marriages have now ended. The pressures are real, whether it is suburban or inner-city America. The sexual revolution has created a problem that the church cannot afford to ignore.

The other side of the sexual revolution is important as well. We can easily stress the negative changes that occurred during the sexual revolution and forget the more positive aspects. The Scripture boldly affirms that human sexuality is a gift from God. When a person uses this God-given capacity rightly, sexual intercourse can be an act of worship. Overcoming the puritanical attitudes often associated with Christianity was the marching cry of the '60s. Christians needed to be put in touch with a more biblically grounded view of sexuality, and the sexual revolution helped to this end. The difficulty is affirming the biblical appreciation of sexuality while not getting caught up in a life-style that distorts God-given parameters.

As we have seen, the sexual revolution increased the pressures felt by teenagers. But these pressures are not limited to teenagers; the growing number of single and single-again persons are faced with tough moral choices as well. All of this simply means that the changes wrought by the sexual revolution should not be ignored. We can choose to sit on the sidelines and decry the excesses, or we can roll up our sleeves and "hammer out" a relevant theology. This will mean more than living by high standards, although the importance of standards cannot be overemphasized. It will mean that we must engage the problems and possibilities created by the sexual revolution.

One notable area of concern is what this means for the church. During the '60s the church became "an institution that meets the needs of society."[7] What the world needs is a church that can combine righteousness and compassion in such a way that it nourishes the moral life. The church should be more than a mirror of secular values. When the church is what God calls it to be, it stands for something, even as it stands with those who feel condemned. The sexual revolution has forced the church to reconsider its role in society.

We have defined the sexual revolution in basic terms. First, the sexual revolution led to a more open discussion of human sexuality. Second, the revolution led to changed attitudes concerning sexuality. Third, the changed terrain argues for an understanding from the church that can combine both righteousness and compassion. The sexual revolution defies any simple definition or analysis. Let us examine the cultural and intellectual forces that have shaped it.

## Cultural Dispositions

Understanding the sexual revolution requires more than describing a series of compromises. There are cultural dispositions that serve as the true indicators of the revolution. A noted Christian ethicist says, "Taking Christian ethics with utmost seriousness requires that we consider the importance of the *ethos,* the social habits, the customs, and laws of any society—whether this be church or civil society."[8] We will look at several attitudes or dispositions that have characterized the 20th century. The premise is that these have helped to create a situation that is conducive to the excesses and insights of the sexual revolution.

**Secular Humanism.** One of the most noticeable features of modern America is the wide acceptance of secular humanism. To retaliate against this philosophy, some evangelical groups have issued a blanket condemnation of everything that bears the label humanism. But a complete rejection of humanism is unnecessary when one considers the full message of the Scripture. First, evangelicals are beginning to understand that humanism encompasses more than secular humanism. A growing and influential number of evangelicals are attempting to recover the significance of humanism for faith.[9] Second, evangelicals are beginning to recognize a latent, if not manifest, humanism in the Hebraic roots of the gospel. Both of these convictions are grounded in the insight of Karl Barth: "[Our] humanity is not blotted out through the fall of man, nor is its goodness diminished."[10] Barth is not accepting the tenets of secular humanism. He seems to be arguing for what could be called evangelical humanism. This brand of humanism is the contemporary mood in much evangelical theology, which seems ready to acknowledge its debts to the Western humanistic tradition, recover an authentic Hebraism, and translate its message into social involvement. The difference

18

between secular humanism and evangelical humanism is the distinction between atheism and the gospel.

According to the *Humanist Manifesto 2,* "The preciousness and dignity of the individual person is a central humanist value."[11] Concerning ethics, the secular humanist believes that "moral values derive their source from human experience."[12] Our time is clearly characterized by the attitude that grounds all value in the individual. The ancient plea of Socrates to "examine oneself" has become the banner under which many march. But Socrates did not look within for ultimate meaning as the secular humanist does. This kind of individualism lies at the center of American culture, but Bellah, a sociologist of religion, is "concerned that this individualism may have grown cancerous."[13] His basic consideration is the cultural effect of individualism, but this has relevance for moral reflection. The human affirmation of moral freedom often becomes moral license and finally moral bondage. The picture painted by Bellah and others is difficult to refute. The attempt to ground all value in humankind has produced not more freedom but more ambiguity for many.

Existentialism has much in common with secular humanism. It is a point of view that seeks to "gather all the elements of human reality into a total picture of man."[14] As a philosophical point of view existentialism is a vigorous attempt to ground value in the individual. This mood pervades much philosophy, theology, literature, art, music, and so on. This disposition is especially evident in the work of Friedrich Nietzsche, who was an opponent of religion and the church. He went to great pains to express the importance of choosing one's own path.

A young man once came up to me after a church service to express his displeasure with something I had said. He was a good-looking individual who was obviously very popular. I had just preached about sexual discipline and the need to control one's sexual appetite. He said, "Such things are personal and have nothing to do with my faith! As long as I do not hurt anybody, why should God care? Besides, you are just expressing church leaders' ideas that have no relevance to me at all." This individual speaks for many in our churches. They are good-looking, talented, and have been nurtured by the ministry of the church. Yet they do not have a clue about the moral implications of the gospel.

**Alienation.** The attempt to ground all value in the self often leads to alienation or "terrifying isolation."[15] We might well heed these insightful words: "Enlightenment killed God; but like Macbeth, the men of the Enlightenment did not know that the cosmos would rebel at the deed, and the world become 'a tale told by an idiot, full of sound and fury, signifying nothing.'"[16] Alienation lies at the end of the road that begins with grounding all value in the self. Slowly even our "life together" begins to disintegrate as we focus more and more on the self. This leads to an alienation that makes us all strangers navigating in the darkness. Here the haunting words of Friedrich Nietzsche are important, "Do we not stray, as through infinite nothingness? Does not empty space breathe upon us?"[17] This reminds me of a T-shirt I saw a young man wearing at Daytona Beach, Fla. Several people had gathered around him to admire his motorcycle. The black T-shirt said, "You have obviously mistaken me for a person who cares!" Unfortunately, this expresses the attitude of many people. Whether such an attitude arises out of profound emotional pain or selfish anger, it is destructive to community. It is, perhaps, the attitude that informed the thinking of a homosexual man who, after being diagnosed as having AIDS, went on to have sex with hundreds of others. Alienation for many leads to the angry affirmation: I am not looking out for others, I am looking out for me!

This terrifying alienation is apparent in *The Trial*, by Franz Kafka. It is a dark novel that begins with the arrest of Joseph K., who is an honest and hardworking citizen. The rest of the novel traces the long and winding path of Joseph K. in his attempt to find out why he was arrested. Toward the end of the story he encounters a priest in the cathedral who tells him a parable. The "parable before the law" begins with a person seeking admission to a door. Before this door stands a doorkeeper, who must grant the privilege of entry. The person asks to enter and is flatly rejected, but with the hint that he will be admitted at a later time. Days and then years go by until the person who sought entry now approaches death. Still he will not be allowed to enter. He asks one final question, "How does it come about . . . that in all these years no one has come seeking admittance but me?"[18] The doorkeeper answers, "No one but you could gain admittance through this door, since this door was intended for you. I am now going to shut it."[19]

This parable is open to many interpretations, but one way to see it is the failure of Joseph K. to act. He freely chose to wait. He might have chosen to die rather than sit patiently and passively before the door for years, even until his own death. One theme of Kafka's work is the necessity of choosing, of acting. A consistent theme of existentialism is the suffering choices humans must make. Such decisions are all the more terrifying when there is no God. This dark terror is epitomized by the famous play *No Exit:* "Dead! Dead! Dead! Knives, poison, ropes—all useless. It has happened *already,* do you understand? Once and for all. So here we are, forever."[20] Such an existence is indeed absurd, perhaps even nauseating.

**Technology.** The existence of science is one of the most significant aspects of modern society. Science can be defined "as the organization of our knowledge in such a way that it commands more of the hidden potential in nature."[21] Bronowski adds further that such a definition of science admits no sharp boundary between knowledge and use."[22] The tremendous advances in science have considerably enhanced the quality of life in much of the world. Simple things like refrigeration have made all of our lives easier. Electricity, the automobile, air travel, the computer, and much more are visible reminders of the contribution that science has made to civilization. Scientific research has improved medical treatment to the point that people generally live happier and healthier lives. No one would dispute the fact that much of what science has done is positive. Although religion has had some notable disputes with the scientific community, each has nourished the other at an even more profound level.

One of the most visible signs of the scientific revolution is technology. Here the emphasis is often placed upon the "how to" capabilities of humanity. Our faith in technology is almost limitless. There is a sense in which technology and science are inseparable in our society. The television, computer, and nuclear weapons symbolize our age: "It has become a general faith, widespread even when it is unvoiced, that technique and technical organization are the necessary and sufficient conditions for arriving at truth; that they can encompass all truth; and that they will be sufficient, if not at the moment, then shortly, to answer the questions that life thrusts upon us."[23]

At the popular level this attitude expresses itself in the 10-minute exercise program or the chemical breakdown diet. The positive thinking authors usually have a very simple plan for our complex problems. Technology has laid very deep tracks into the mind-set of our time. This is so much the case that people often learn how to operate something instead of understanding how something operates. This fact was made plain to me by the comment of a gentleman in a Sunday School class. He said, "I may not know how the light switch works, but I know it works every time." Yet, if we will think a minute about this statement, we will see that somebody has to understand the principle. It is not healthy to turn off our minds because we always get light when the switch is flipped.

Technology is important to the sexual revolution for many reasons. First, because of medical research it is possible to experiment more safely. The birth control pill and even safer abortion procedures have led many to conclude that premarital sex is risk-free. Second, some are led to conclude that whatever disease results from sexual intercourse can be successfully treated with drugs. Third, our greater awareness through mass media of alternative life-styles has eroded any consensus about what is or is not moral. Fourth, our greater mobility gives people an opportunity to experiment sexually. The automobile is in many ways a moving motel room that teens in previous generations did not have. For example, my parents took the bus for their dates; it looks like today's children will use conversion vans. All of these depend to a large extent upon technology. H. Ray Dunning reminds us, "The Christian understanding is that while such discoveries or inventions are a gift of God, they must be seen as servants rather than masters."[24] Technology challenges us to examine our faith.

The Scripture records a very interesting story that is relevant to our understanding of technology. Gen. 11:1-9 describes a tower the people attempted to build. The purpose of this tower is expressed clearly: "Let us build ourselves a city, with a tower that reaches to the heavens, so that we may make a name for ourselves and not be scattered over the face of the whole earth" (v. 4). The story illustrates God's judgment upon humankind's attempt to be self-sufficient. The people had the confidence that they could reach God with purely human efforts. The tower would take the place of God and would establish their identity.

On January 28, 1986, many Americans were shaken as the news reported that the space shuttle *Challenger* had exploded. It was with an attitude of disbelief that some admitted technology had failed. Others blamed the whole thing on human error, because it would be too painful to suggest that technology was insufficient. Yet those haunting clouds of smoke are an inescapable reminder that humankind's best knowledge is inadequate.

Since the sexual revolution coincided with the rise of technology, people had the means to more safely express themselves sexually. But this has left the larger question unanswered: "Should I do this at all?" It is a question not of whether one gets away with the act but of whether it is right. Technology can cause the moral question to recede into the background. Perhaps one of the greatest challenges will be to recover the importance of the moral question. The fact "We can do it" must not become more important than the question "Should we do it?"

Technology is a mixed blessing for most of us. It makes our lives easier and healthier. But it could also end our lives in a nuclear cloud. The increased share of time afforded by technology should give us more time to humanize our world, but it often becomes a tool that accomplishes the opposite. Technology has given many the impression that "ability to do something amounts to condoning it." Along with this has come the idea that "whatever pain results from my actions is curable through technology." Neither of these is true, but for many this knowledge has come too late. Technology is not a one-way ticket to the good life, rather it is a tool that helps improve the quality of life.

**Pluralism.** Doubtless the most powerful force in American life is the acceptance of multiple perspectives. Because we have tried to ground all value in the self, we have developed a tendency to regard all ideas as equally valid. The alienation that has all too often separated us from one another has led us to affirm almost anything that brings even a little light. Recently I saw a television reporter ask an elderly lady a pointed question. She was attending a political rally where her congressman had just announced that he was a practicing homosexual. When asked about her thoughts, she responded, "I don't want anybody to judge me; I am not going to judge anybody." Pluralism is the acceptance of all truth as more or less equal. What the lady expressed may be a little lazy, but it grows out of the moral climate of our day. The television talk show is the happy haven of pluralism, at the popular level. Such programs often espouse the view that intensity of belief or even commitment are the sole criteria of truth.

The hallmark of pluralism is the rejection of all authority. It is easy to see how this relates to the mood created by existentialism. Many view religion as the last bastion of authoritarianism. The church is rejected as an institution that needs to be transcended. Some go so far as to call the church "morally hypocritical."[25] The church responds to this in several ways; one is to become more authoritarian. We can see this mood in much fundamentalism, chiefly illustrated by many television evangelists. The sad reality of the last several years is the discovery that some of these men "only preached the message." A second response is an easy accommodation of the secular point of view. Bloom reminds us, *"Secularization* is the wonderful mechanism by which religion becomes nonreligion."[26]

I would like to propose a third approach, characterized by an attempt to ground our theology in Scripture and at the same time to be relevant. This kind of response would constantly be about the task of hearing the radical word of deliverance in the Scripture and expressing that message clearly.

Another characteristic of pluralism is relativism. This is the theory that ideas of what are right and good depend on the individual or groups holding them. Relativism implies that no universal norms exist. Moderate relativism can be helpful because it opens one's mind to new ideas. Radical relativism is dangerous because it leads one to conclude that all truth is equal. American culture and even some evangelical Christians are moving toward the more dangerous manifestation of relativism. The Early Church fathers never doubted that they were proclaiming the "one true way." In fact, Paul's one notable attempt to preach the gospel to philosophers was a dismal failure (Acts 17:16-34; 1 Cor. 1:18 —2:15). Erasmus in the spirit of the Renaissance sought to reduce the gospel to a set of philosophical propositions. The church has, however, followed the insights of Martin Luther with more enthusiasm. His "theology of the Cross" has captured the message of the gospel with more clarity and power. Christian morality must be grounded in some absolutes; relativism makes a strange partner for Christianity.

Radical openness also characterizes pluralism. The rejection of all authority and the relativism that follows is always accompanied by such an openness. A friend of mine has a saying that amuses as it instructs: "Don't be so open-minded that your brains fall out!" This is a subtle reminder that everything one hears is not equally valid. It is also a call to be "tough-minded." This will enable a person to stand for something; it will require being against some things. William Willimon wrote an article a number of years ago in which he reminded the reader that often what sells for kindness is actually cowardice in disguise.[27] Most of those in the evangelical church could stand a little open-mindedness; but this should not be an excuse for the attitude that says, "Just as long as you believe it is true, it is."

Pluralism is expressed in the rejection of authority, in relativism, and in radical openness. The sexual revolution is quite comfortable with these ideas and has to a large extent lived them out. It has led many to openly espouse sexual behavior once thought to be immoral. It has allowed some to write that love between homosexuals can be holy love.[28] Karen Lebacqz argues for the morality of sexual intercourse among singles on the basis of vulnerability. She says, "We need a theology of vulnerability. Until a theology is forthcoming, we can only struggle toward a proper sexual ethic."[29] She goes on to argue for premarital, postmarital, gay, and lesbian union on the basis of this principle. All of this makes perfect sense to the culture of pluralism, but it leaves the evangelical Christian mystified.

One more effect of pluralism needs to be briefly noted. Some describe our time as postmodern. Mark C. Taylor, one of the foremost exponents of this position, talks about "having interiorized the death of God."[30] He further states that "we must learn to speak of God godlessly or of the self selflessly."[31] Taylor clearly understands that his vision of theology arises out of the culture of pluralism. He expresses this more clearly in a later book, *Erring: A Postmodern A/Theology:* "The echoes of the death of God can be heard in the disappearance of the self, the end of history, and the closure of the book."[32] This represents one of the growing edges of theology. It is a clear example of the direction pluralism can take religion. This works its way into morality by the "absurd freedom" of Sartre. Here we are forced to choose our path without any divine direction. Perhaps it is better referred to as "a freedom held in bondage to the self."

We have dealt with four cultural dispositions. They are interrelated through the ambiguities already present today. Secular humanism, alienation, technology, and pluralism have created an environment ready-made for the sexual revolution. In fact, apart from the world indicated by these dispositions, much of the sexual revolution would have been impossible. They have helped to free people of previous inhibitions but not to prepare them for a more human existence. I would maintain that such meaning is only possible in an ethic grounded in the gospel of our Lord Jesus Christ. The remainder of this book will be an attempt to set forth this gospel, for "those who obey his commands live in him, and he in them" (1 John 3:24).

This chapter is based upon the premise that many of the excesses of the sexual revolution are over. Herpes, syphilis, AIDS, and other realities have dampened the rhetoric of freedom that originally accompanied the revolution. Some studies are indicating that a higher percentage of our college youth are choosing to remain virgins. Others suggest that college students hold more conservative values than in the previous two decades. Even the "hippies" and "yippies" of the '60s and '70s have become the "yuppies" of the '80s. All of this could lead to the false impression that the revolution failed and everything has returned to a pre-'60s mentality. We must not confuse political conservatism with Christian morality. Hopefully, the material included in this chapter is sufficient to show how much has changed and continues to change. The challenge before the Christian is clear: "[to] contend for the faith which was once delivered unto the saints" (Jude 3, KJV). These words are all the more powerful when we understand they were written to warn against those "who change the grace of our God into a license for immorality" (Jude 4). We must find a way of living out the gospel in these times.

The next three chapters will set forth three principles for untangling the sexual revolution: self-respect, the meaning of love, and responsible freedom. Basic to my approach is that it is time to search out the most fundamental resources of the gospel for Christian living. A person loses nothing and gains a great deal by building life on the sure foundation of Christ. Our young people do not need more arguments against immoral sexual behavior, because most of these have been tried already. There is rather a crying need for an early and persistent attempt to lay the right foundation. Do we really believe that a child who is raised in the fear of the Lord will not finally depart from it? I suggest that the real work of ethics is theological. It is sharing the rich resources of the Christian tradition for sexual existence.

The following pages are a joyous attempt to express one pilgrim's grappling with the challenge of the sexual revolution. I write this book not only for myself but also for our children, who have inherited a world where the "loss of our deeper or primal identity"[33] threatens to overcome us all.

## Summary

1. While the excesses of the sexual revolution appear to be moderating, a deeper, more profound change is just beginning.

2. The sexual revolution refers to that period of American life that led to a more open and informed discussion of sexuality.

3. Changed views on sexuality, increased pressures on the young, and a more positive understanding of sexuality have grown out of the sexual revolution.

4. The sexual revolution has grown out of certain cultural dispositions: secular humanism, alienation, technology, pluralism.

## Notes

1. Donald Dayton, *Discovering an Evangelical Heritage* (New York: Harper and Row, Publishers, 1976), 1.

2. James B. Nelson, "Reuniting Sexuality and Spirituality," *Christian Century* (Feb. 25, 1987): 190.

3. Leonard Sweet, "The 1960s: The Crises of Liberal Christianity and the Public Emergence of Evangelicalism," in *Evangelicalism and Modern America,* ed. George Marsden (Grand Rapids: William B. Eerdmans Publishing Co., 1984), 30.

4. Allan Bloom, *The Closing of the American Mind: How Higher Education Has Failed Democracy and Impoverished the Souls of Today's Students* (New York: Simon and Schuster, 1987), 98.

5. David Mace, *The Christian Response to the Sexual Revolution* (Nashville: Abingdon Press, 1970), 68.

6. Allen Moore, "Teen-age Sexuality and Public Morality," *Christian Century* (Sept. 9, 1987): 747.

7. Sweet, "The 1960s," 31.

8. Paul Ramsey, "On Taking Sexual Responsibility Seriously Enough," in *Social Ethics: Issues in Ethics and Society,* ed. Gibson Winter (New York: Harper and Row, Publishers, 1968), 53.

9. Several books recently published by evangelical presses and written by respected evangelicals lead me to this conclusion: Ray Anderson, *On Being Human: Essays in Theological Anthropology;* Paul Brand and Philip Yancey, *In His Image;* Arthur Holmes, *All Truth Is God's Truth;* J. I. Packer and Thomas Howard, *Christianity: The True Humanism.*

10. Karl Barth, *The Humanity of God,* trans. John Thomas (Atlanta: John Knox Press, 1960, 1976), 53.

11. Paul Kurtz, ed., *Humanist Manifesto 1 and 2* (Buffalo, N.Y.: Prometheus Books, 1973), 18.

12. Ibid., 17.

13. Robert Bellah et al., *Habits of the Heart: Individualism and Commitment in American Life* (New York: Harper and Row, Publishers, 1985), vii.

14. William Barrett, *Irrational Man: A Study in Existential Philosophy* (Garden City, N.Y.: Doubleday and Co., 1958, 1962), 21.

15. Ibid., 6.

16. Bloom, *Closing,* 196.

17. Friedrich Nietzsche, "The Death of God," in *The New Christianity: An Anthology of the Rise of Modern Religious Thought,* ed. William Miller (New York: Dell Publishing Co., 1967), 139.

18. Franz Kafka, *The Trial,* trans. Willa and Edwin Muir (New York: Schocken Books, 1925, 1968), 214.

19. Ibid., 214-15.

20. Jean-Paul Sartre, *No Exit and Three Other Plays* (New York: Vintage Books, 1955), 47.

21. J. Bronowski, *Science and Human Values* (New York: Harper and Row, Publishers, 1956, 1965), 7.

22. Ibid.

23. William Barrett, *The Illusion of Technique: A Search for Meaning in a Technological Civilization* (Garden City, N.Y.: Anchor Press, Doubleday, 1979), 10-11.

24. H. Ray Dunning, "Holiness, Technology, and Personhood," *Wesleyan Theological Journal* 21, nos. 1 and 2 (Spring-Fall 1986): 183.

25. Bellah, *Habits,* 64.

26. Bloom, *Closing,* 211.

27. William Willimon, "The Limits of Kindness," *Christian Century* (Apr. 14, 1982): 447-49.

28. John J. McNeill, "Homosexuality: Challenging the Church to Grow," *Christian Century* (Mar. 11, 1987): 243.

29. Karen Lebacqz, "Appropriate Vulnerability: A Sexual Ethic of Singles," *Christian Century* (May 6, 1987): 438.

30. Mark C. Taylor, *De-Constructing Theology* (New York: Crossroad Publishing Co., 1982), xx.

31. Ibid., 89.

32. Mark C. Taylor, *Erring: A Postmodern A/Theology* (Chicago and London: University of Chicago Press, 1984), 8.

33. Thomas J. J. Altizer, *History as Apocalypse* (Albany, N.Y.: State University of New York Press, 1985), 7; see n. 11.

# 2

# Self-respect

I am worth something! This may sound like a cocky affirmation of a person drunk with self-importance. Actually, it is the affirmation of Scripture (Gen. 1:31). An understanding of self-respect, as it is taught in the Bible, is essential in our attempt to untangle the sexual revolution. One message that has been sounded during this time is that humankind is little more than an extension of the animal world. Phil Donahue's week-long television special "The Human Animal" attempts to understand human sexuality by studying the mating habits that characterize the animal kingdom. During the program he interviews several researchers. One says it is unrealistic to expect humans to be faithful to one another, given increased life expectancy, perhaps as high as the 80s. The hidden premise of this exercise is that human sexual patterns are not significantly different from those of the animal kingdom. Indeed, from a biological or even anthropological point of view this may seem warranted. But Scripture is clear that while God created all good things, humankind is called to moral responsibility in a way that the rest of creation is not (Gen. 2:15-17). Self-respect is a biblically grounded principle that establishes the meaning of moral responsibility.

Not long ago when boarding an airplane for a flight from Atlanta to Boston, I noticed a mother and her young daughter. They struggled a bit but finally found a seat several rows behind me. Since we have a little girl who is about this age, it was almost amusing to see the two prepare for takeoff. Suddenly the mother screamed at the little girl, "You are nothing but a pain! You are worthless!" I did not turn to see the face of the little girl, but certainly she was emotionally damaged. It made me hurt for the girl and to some extent for the mother. Perhaps you are saying that I am taking the incident too seriously. I think not. What did the little girl hear? What was she thinking? What will she remember? How often will she have to hear it before she believes it? Too many people are held in bondage to low self-respect. This can lead to a dulled sense of moral responsibility. If I am worthless, then what I do with my body or to the bodies of other people is unimportant.

The world is full of people who believe they do not count. Perhaps they were told as children or have come to believe it as adults. Far too often personal worth is linked to the size of one's bank account. Other times it is tied up with physical attractiveness or popularity. The liberating word of the gospel is that every human being is of eternal value. Self-respect is a biblically grounded truth with profound implications for moral reflection.

## The Doctrine of Creation

Ps. 33:6 proclaims, "By the word of the Lord were the heavens made, their starry host by the breath of his mouth." This is just one example of many statements in Scripture that testify to the importance of understanding creation. This doctrine is central to the Christian faith. Further, understanding this truth, as taught in Scripture, is essential to moral reflection. The next several pages will attempt to lay out the importance of this doctrine for untangling the sexual revolution.

Self-respect is a concept, perhaps an affirmation, that grows out of the doctrine of creation. Three bold assertions accompany the biblical message concerning creation: God is the Creator, creation is good, and the final purpose of everything is to glorify God. The thought underlying all of this is that God is the point of origin for all that is good. It also suggests that the doctrine of creation opens up new levels of understanding: morally and theologically. Three biblical concepts—the image of God, the temple of the Holy Spirit, and the Resurrection—relate to creation and have relevance for moral reflection.

Before we look at these three concepts, it is necessary to mention the darker side of creation. Scripture is very clear in its affirmation of the essential goodness of humanity. This is the most basic fact concerning human existence. There is, however, a companion doctrine that illuminates the meaning of creation: the doctrine of the Fall. Adam, the first man, is driven out of the Garden of Eden (Gen. 3:24). When Paul speaks of it, he paints a very dark picture of humanity: "For although they knew God, they neither glorified him as God nor gave thanks to him, but their thinking became futile and their foolish hearts were darkened" (Rom. 1:21). Later in Romans, Paul makes it very clear exactly what he is saying: "Death reigned from the time of Adam to the time of Moses, even over those who did not sin by breaking a command, as did Adam, who was a pattern of the one to come" (5:14). The Fall is a dark and painful indication of what happens when a being intended to glorify God turns away from light and life toward darkness and death. It means that the person who could live in "love, joy, peace, patience, kindness, goodness, faithfulness, gentleness and self-control" (Gal. 5:22-23) has chosen and chooses "sexual immorality, impurity and debauchery; idolatry and witchcraft; hatred, discord, jealousy . . . orgies, and the like" (vv. 19-21) instead. Humankind is a "being of light," but the Scripture tells us that there is a resistance (or a revolt) in this being that brings darkness. We could have enjoyed perfect fellowship with God (in the light), but we have all chosen and do choose darkness. This is certainly one of the great mysteries of life.

We must not get carried away with this scenario of darkness, for ultimately "through the obedience of the one man the many will be made righteous" (Rom. 5:19). The final word concerning humankind is not about darkness, death, and sin, but light, life, and righteousness. The Christian should look for whatever is good, noble, brave, and redemptive in the world. Because self-respect is central to the Scripture, it becomes our responsibility to look for the flicker of light amid the manifold darkness. It is comforting that even a little light dispels a great deal of darkness. We can say with John, "We have seen his glory, the glory of the One and Only, who came from the Father, full of grace and truth" (John 1:14). This is glory that shines through the lives of the redeemed.

**The Image of God.** According to Gen. 1:27, "God created man in his own image, in the image of God he created him; male and female he created them." These very powerful words translate into the biblically grounded understanding of self-respect. Humankind as created in the image of God posits a relationship (God and humankind). It means that there "is a fellowship of creation and the human being is a member of it."[1] At the most fundamental level God and humankind have a special relationship; this translates into responsibility. Accordingly, "humans are to correspond to God so that something can happen between them and God, so that God can speak to them and they can answer."[2]

Another aspect of this image is freedom. Bonhoeffer says, "In man God creates his image on earth. This means that man is like the Creator in that he is free."[3] Essentially this means that human beings are free to choose. The principles that assume the greatest significance in our life are for the most part our decision. Perhaps it is also important to suggest that this freedom is "a relationship and nothing else."[4] Human beings have freedom only when a positive and growing relationship with God exists. This relationship is described by Paul: "You have been set free from sin and have become slaves to righteousness" (Rom. 6:18). This is part of the plan of God to renew His image in humankind.

Being created in the image of God means that "the human being is God's indirect manifestation on earth."[5] A human being can mirror God's creative intent. James Gustafson stresses that once we have decided what God is, it becomes our responsibility to reflect that in the world. He says, "The first ethical question is never 'What ought we to do?' It is, 'What is God doing?'"[6] Once we have discovered what God is like, it is our responsibility to reflect that insight. First Pet. 1:15 indicates this: "But just as he who called you is holy, so be holy in all you do." The testimony of the Scripture is that humanity should reflect God.

A final aspect of the image of God is moral responsibility. According to Moltmann, the German theologian, "Finally, human beings are created for the sabbath, to reflect and praise the glory of God which enters into creation, and takes up its dwelling there."[7] The New Testament declares, "Since the promise of entering his rest still stands, let us be careful that none of you be found to have fallen short of it" (Heb. 4:1). The sabbath refers to a life controlled by the sense of God's presence; this is moral responsibility.

**The Temple of the Holy Spirit.** One of the most astounding truths of the Scripture is that as human beings we have the capacity to bear the Holy Spirit. Redeemed humanity, both as individuals and as the Church, bear the Spirit. "Believers are in Christ not only as individuals but as a people."[8] Paul asks the church at Corinth, "Do you not know that your body is a temple of the Holy Spirit, who is in you, whom you have received from God?" (1 Cor. 6:19). The promise of the Scripture is that as Christians we can live as children of the light. This sets the Christian apart to a better kind of life.

The Church is composed of those who have been called out of the world into fellowship with God. This community as the bearer of the Spirit brings hope, dignity, and love to a world that needs all three. The plain fact is that the Holy Spirit dwells in the Church as a whole, but in such a manner that each believer is the temple of the Holy Spirit.

The argument of Paul is clear at this point: Our body is meant to glorify the Lord. We have been delivered from the immoral use of the body by the power of the Resurrection and have been joined together with Christ. We are part of Him, and He is part of us. It is, perhaps, a bit startling, but sexual immorality is likened to joining the body of Christ to a prostitute (1 Cor. 6:15). Paul's illustration has profound moral significance. "Flee from sexual immorality. All other sins a man commits are outside his body, but he who sins sexually sins against his own body" (v. 18). Sexual sin goes to the very soul of a human being. Since we are the temple of the Holy Spirit, we should honor God with our body.

Along with this principle Paul adds another thought: "Everything is permissible" (v. 12). This is a surprising idea because it sounds a great deal like much of the rhetoric of the sexual revolution. A misunderstanding of it could lead to the conclusion that we can do anything we want for as long as we want! Such a view fails to see the real point being made by Paul.

The affirmation of the gospel is freedom. Love God and do as you will is a thoroughly Christian understanding of moral responsibility. Christian ethics is not about rules and restrictions built upon more rules and more restrictions. Christianity is really about being touched by a love so great that it opens one up to a new life. This freedom, which can only be found in Christ, is real, not just apparent. Two insights arise out of this truth: "Not everything is beneficial" and "I will not be mastered by anything" (1 Cor. 6:12). So much that sells itself as liberation is really bondage in disguise. First, we must learn to ask about consequences. What will this do to other people? Does my action bring a brighter future or the reverse? The Christian life is not about getting away with sin, but living the highest and purest possible kind of existence (Matt. 5:6, 8). "Not everything is beneficial"; and for one who bears the Spirit, that is an important consideration. Second, we must learn to ask about what controls us. Too many actions are dictated by appetite. A popular television commercial depicts a person who has a "Big Mac Attack." This person drops everything in order to consume a hamburger. This is an amusing advertisement, but some seem to think that sexual appetite is analogous. For those who bear the Spirit, the consuming desire is to be characterized by God's presence.

This concept, "Everything is permissible," does not abolish our responsibility but deepens it. This will require a level of honesty that the law could never mandate. It will force us to see what it is that we really want, to see ourselves as we really are. Several years ago I received a telephone call from a college student. He expressed his frustration with trying to control himself sexually while on a date. He was quick to say that he respected his girlfriend, but he just could not control himself. It was easy during the week because he worked hard at his studies, plus he had a part-time job. But the weekend was another matter. They would always end the date with a couple of hours of parking in a secluded spot. The first hour would be fine, but the second hour always brought trouble. It was plain to see that he was not being honest. They both intended to have sexual intercourse by planning the time for it to happen. An ethic that is defined by the Holy Spirit will force us to look deep into our souls, to examine our motives.

**Resurrection.** The third example of how creation is important in the Scripture is the Resurrection. Perhaps there is no single idea that is more important in the New Testament. Understood in its fullest sense "the resurrection of Christ directs our attention back to the creation which it vindicates."[9] The purpose here is not to fully explicate the theological significance of this concept, but rather to see how it supports the broad biblical understanding of self-respect.

First Corinthians 15 is pivotal to any theological treatment of the Resurrection. Paul begins the chapter by summarizing the Christian gospel (vv. 3-8) around this theme. Alan Richardson reflects upon redemption in Christ: "The original unity or harmony of things, which was disrupted on a cosmic scale by man's fall into sin, is now being restored by Christ's redeeming work; and what had hitherto existed in a state of separation or even enmity is now being unified in the new-created wholeness of Christ."[10] For Paul, the Resurrection establishes the gospel (v. 29). It gives meaning to our lives and our proclamation of the faith. It leads him to say that "by the grace of God I am what I am, and his grace to me was not without effect" (v. 10). This grace compels Paul toward a ministry of reconciliation (2 Cor. 5:11-21). Accordingly, "The new life of believers is not a matter that can be known or approached out of the inwardness of the spiritual life, but only out of what has taken place in Christ's death and resurrection."[11]

The Resurrection means that we have a new life. The gospel begins at creation, but it surely focuses on the new life in Jesus Christ. This theme of deliverance can be noted in a number of places in the Scripture. According to Richardson, "Since the salvation wrought by God at the exodus was thought of as an act of new creation involving again a deliverance from the power of the deep, it is not surprising that we find in the New Testament the representation of salvation in Christ as like an act of new creation and of the defeat of the powers of evil."[12] Second Cor. 5:17 says, "Therefore, if anyone is in Christ, he is a new creation; the old has gone, the new has come!" This well-known affirmation is important to the kind of moral reflection that begins in self-respect.

The Resurrection means that we may have new power. In Jesus Christ not only are we made new, but also we are given power to be all that God intends for us to be. The Christian is called to a new life; we are invited to partake of a new power. God not only pulls us out of the old life but also gives us the resources to live a better kind of existence. The comprehensive term used by Paul is "in Christ." "It is Christ in the believer that assures him of the hope of final redemption."[13] This kind of assurance comes from knowing that the resurrected Lord is with us.

The Resurrection means that we must bring life. The gospel is the message that we must bear. Paul says it this way: "The sting of death is sin, and the power of sin is the law. But thanks be to God! He gives us the victory through our Lord Jesus Christ" (1 Cor. 15:56-57). Self-respect includes the power to accept love and to share it. Paul Tillich tells a story in a sermon titled "The Power of Love" of a woman who established an orphanage in Europe during the terrible days of World War II. Eventually she ministered to children of many people who had died in the war on both sides of the conflict. He says about her: "It is a rare gift to meet a human being in whom love—and this means God—is so overwhelmingly manifest . . . It is more than justice and it is greater than faith and hope. It is the presence of God himself. For God is love. And in every moment of genuine love we are dwelling in God and God in us."[14]

These three ideas—the image of God, the temple of the Holy Spirit, and the Resurrection—are powerful reminders of self-respect. If we are ever going to untangle the sexual revolution, it will be necessary to understand who we are in God's creation. Self-respect opens us to the biblical affirmation of human sexuality.

## The Mystery of Human Sexuality

Deeply grounded in the biblical understanding of humankind is the mystery of human sexuality. Solomon praises such an understanding of physical love in the Song of Songs. A fully orbed treatment of humanity must include sexuality, for it is not just a dimension of existence; it lies at the center. Self-respect grows out of an appreciation of creation, but it extends to a full-blown affirmation of human sexuality.

**A Good Gift.** The clear teaching of the Scriptures is that human sexuality is a gift of God. For too long the mystery and joy of sexuality have been hidden under layers of misunderstanding. This has led many to a certain uneasiness about sexuality, perhaps even guilt. Gen. 1:27 states, "Male and female he created them." This certainly suggests that "our human sexuality is God's good gift. It is a fundamental dimension of our created and our intended humanness."[15] Sexuality is not a curse to be borne but a gift to be cherished. It is one way that we can better understand our walk with God: "When sex is seen in this wide context, it cannot be regarded as an isolated biological phenomenon which has no relation to our social situation; neither can it be seen as a simple urge which we share with the other animals."[16]

James Nelson develops four "interwoven themes [that] assist . . . in seeing the significance of the sexual body to Christian theology."[17] These themes are feeling, desiring, communion, and incarnation.[18] He contends, therefore, that human sexuality opens up new levels of understanding for the Christian. Because sexuality is a gift, "The act in itself is *good.* It can *never* be altogether *evil,* since it is a part of God's good creation, but it can be so distorted in its functioning that it

38

becomes *instrumentally* evil."[19] To avoid the evil distortions of sexuality, we must first understand its goodness.

A Christian counselor once told me of a very beautiful woman who sought advice. She had been married for several years but had found no sexual fulfillment. Her husband was a loving, tender, and compassionate man. Yet they had not found intercourse to be enjoyable. After a number of months, the counselor discovered a part of the problem. The woman had been raised in a Christian home, but her parents had been forced to get married because of pregnancy. It was her father's great fear that his daughter would end up in the same kind of trouble. He began at an early age to tell her that all boys wanted one thing. She carried this negative predisposition into her marriage. Even within the bounds of God's intended expression of sexual intimacy, she could not enjoy the good gift of sexuality. After years of counseling the woman began to understand that her sexuality is a gift.

This story should encourage each of us to be very careful about the way human sexuality is interpreted for the young. It is possible that in our desire to teach our children to avoid sexual immorality, we will unwittingly distort the Christian message. The final word concerning human sexuality in the Christian tradition is not condemnation but one of blessing.

While it is true that Scripture affirms human sexuality, it is also true that the Christian faith has not always reflected this. There has been, almost from the beginning, a tendency to treat sexuality in a negative way. Augustine is a fifth-century theologian who represents this tendency. He says in *The Confessions*, "Love and lust together seethed within me. In my tender youth they swept me away over the precipice of my body's appetites and plunged me in the whirlpool of sin . . . I was tossed and spilled, floundering in the broiling sea of my fornication."[20] This very negative message is apparent throughout Augustine's work. Thomas Aquinas approximately 700 years later is very dependent upon Augustine for his analysis of human sexuality. He separates the desires of the soul and the body in such a way that sexual desire is linked to the senses as opposed to reason.[21] When sexuality is treated in such a way, it becomes merely a passion to be controlled. Thus, sexuality is a necessary evil, but never a good gift of God to be enjoyed.

A proper understanding of human sexuality will require that we look beyond the pessimistic images that often have dominated the Christian tradition. The words of Scripture tell another story: "May your fountain be blessed, and may you rejoice in the wife of your youth. A loving doe, a graceful deer—may her breasts satisfy you always, may you ever be captivated by her love" (Prov. 5:18-19). A noted theologian reminds us, "Sexuality, when rightly used and properly enjoyed, is a sharing in the love of God himself for His creation."[22]

Why has Christianity so often held a negative view of sexuality? Perhaps the best explanation of this is the influence of Greek philosophy on Christianity. The Greeks, in an attempt to accentuate the virtues of the soul, tended to denigrate the body. They viewed the body as a sort of prison for the soul. This view is most evident in Stoic philosophy, which taught the necessity of detachment from external circumstances. It is also seen in Plato's teachings, which contended that reality is nonsensible and that the world of sense is little more than a shadow. Christians picked up these messages very early and began to link spirituality with a detachment from the physical. Withdrawing from the world has been the usual paradigm for true spirituality. Passages in Paul like Phil. 4:11-12 seem to confirm this interpretation. According to Donald Berry, "It is not accidental that the mainstream of Western theological tradition seems to have had so little to say about the empirical human situation."[23] A gospel that seeks to grow out of the Old Testament faith will be more in touch with the body. Berry says, "Being in touch with the body will bring us reports of sensuous pleasure, warmth, good feelings—not to be denied or suppressed; not to be apologized for; not a source of religious embarrassment."[24] Recognizing that human sexuality is a good gift will require that we become more Hebraic in our understanding of the gospel.

Sexuality is a gift of God; it is essential to a solid understanding of human nature. It is one way to participate in

God's creation according to His intention. The pessimistic view of sexuality will be overcome as we more fully recover the meaning of creation and self-respect. It is possible to be fully alive, in touch with our sexuality and seriously devoted to the spiritual quest. Sexuality "is the concrete manifestation of the divine call to completion, a call extended to every person in the very act of creation."[25] An ethic of self-respect will allow one to affirm his body as a gift. This affirmation will allow the goodness of God to be exercised in the living out of the gospel. This is the true meaning of self-respect.

**Centrality.** Even a cursory reading of the New Testament will reveal the importance attached to sexual behavior. Col. 3:5 is one example: "Put to death, therefore, whatever belongs to your earthly nature: sexual immorality, impurity, lust, evil desires." Similar admonitions are apparent in 1 Cor. 5:11; 6:9-10; Gal. 5:19-21; and Eph. 5:3. These biblical passages illustrate the seriousness with which the Christian faith addresses sexuality. It is not possible to separate one's sexual behavior from living out the gospel.

A former classmate of mine developed an interesting view of theology and sexuality. He was a brilliant student who read theology with a vigor unmatched by almost anyone. I was surprised when, one night as we talked around a dining room table, he told me that in his opinion morality and theology had nothing to do with one another. He explained that this was a breath of fresh air for him, since he was raised in a conservative church. His reading of theology had freed him from the bondage of legalism, and finally of the moral imperative present in the gospel. As he defended his view, he informed me that he was sexually involved with his girlfriend. This was a beautiful relationship that had rather naturally been consummated in sexual intercourse. How could anything that feels so right be wrong? Because of this situation he had decided that theology did not include any moral claims. Such a separation is untenable and even dangerous to the Christian faith. When one attempts to separate the moral life from the Christian faith that nourishes it, everything else suffers. When a person seeks to determine moral standards,

41

there must be a place to stand. For me, that place is the Christian tradition with all of its centuries of explanation. What my friend was attempting to do would eventually cause him to reject any real faith at all.

The mystery of human sexuality is in part indicated by its centrality to Christian ethics. Perhaps the first momentous moral dilemma faced by anyone involves sexuality. Issues like lying, stealing, or cheating come earlier for some, but the issue of sexuality arises at the point in life when one must take a measure of responsibility for consequences. The Scripture makes it clear that sexual expression has moral implications. Therefore it is important to get one's sexual life together with one's Christian life.[26] It is undoubtedly true that "a person cannot treat sex as a purely biological need without seriously endangering its total value and meaning in his life."[27] According to Lisa Cahill, a feminist theologian, " 'Sexuality' is 'morality.' "[28]

**Personhood.** According to Lewis Smedes, "Sexuality refers to what we are, not only what we do."[29] This suggests that personhood and sexuality must be considered together. Many of the most pressing issues concerning human sexuality relate to our understanding of personhood. Attempts, both Christian and non-Christian, to combine personhood with human sexuality are apparent in our time. There are five distinct approaches to the question of human sexuality and personhood.

1. One attempt to resolve the question of personhood is to suggest that male and female are equal. I am not referring to civil or political rights but to the attempt to erase all social roles as they relate to sexuality. A female is not different from a male in any way that really counts. This view asserts that all sexual and social roles are learned, thus they can be corrected: "To emancipate woman is to refuse to confine her to the relations she bears to man, not to deny them to her; let her have her independent existence and she will continue nonetheless to exist for him also: mutually recognizing each other as subject, each will yet remain for the other an *other.*"[30] For those who hold this view, sexuality is discarded

as a significant factor in all human relationships. It should be obvious that such a view argues for the morality of homosexual love.

2. Chauvinism represents another attempt to resolve the relationship between personhood and sexuality. For many this view is the Christian understanding, plain and simple. Aquinas felt that a female was a misbegotten male, less dignified than a man, and was the occasion for the fall of man. Calvin argued that a woman is subordinated by creation. Luther saw the chief function of women to be child rearing.[31] This view holds that man is superior to woman, at least for matters of leadership and decision making. Eph. 5:22-33 is often used to support chauvinism. Here women are told to submit to their husbands (v. 22) in everything (v. 24). Even in the following verses (vv. 25-33), where husbands are told to love their wives as their own bodies, a certain paternalism is present. This suggests that women need men for protection and care. Some would argue that such a position "excludes [the] woman and her nature."[32] The arguments are fierce on either side of this issue.

The chauvinistic approach has a long tradition. It is evident in some Christian books on marriage, where the wife is taught "how to" submit. It is evident in those cultures, both Western and Eastern, where the physical strength of the male is understood to place the female in a less-privileged class. It is also suggested when the female is responsible to hide the body in order to keep from tempting the male. It is present whenever females are made to bear the burden of sexual innuendo.

3. A third option is feminism, which "seeks to find the root of the alienation that has created the sexist image of the self and society."[33] There is no easy way to categorize the modern women's movement, because no one person speaks for all women. Feminism can be so radical as to call all men "deficient [and] emotionally limited."[34] In its more moderate manifestations, feminism can be traced to an interest in understanding and fully appreciating the contributions made by women. Feminism, at least in its moderate form, is consistent with evangelical Christianity.

The contribution of feminism to the discussion concerning sexuality and personhood is significant. First, women bring to all relationships a valuable point of view. A fully human perspective will necessarily include a feminine principle. Second, any denigration of women impacts sexual expression by an inadequate understanding of personhood. Third, an adequate view of personhood will include a worldview where the differences between male and female are recognized and allowed to complement each other.

4. Marriage is another way to deal with the question of personhood and sexuality. According to Lewis Smedes, "The male and female know themselves only in relation to each other because they are made for each other."[35] Since sexual expression is so central to the meaning of personhood, and the only appropriate place to express such intimacy is marriage, it follows that this is the only true path to wholeness.

According to this view both men and women are in the image of God. There is no real point of talking about which sex is superior to the other. The focus is upon fidelity and growth as they bond a relationship. Only in the context of marriage do a man and a woman become all that God intended. There is much evidence to commend this view, but one significant problem exists. It carries a subtle implication that one is fully human only through the sexual act. Could it be that we are not fully persons until, in the context of marriage, sexual intercourse has taken place? If this were the case, it would deny full humanity to anyone who is not married.

5. One final attempt to combine sexuality and personhood is shared humanity. This view simply asserts that the two sexes are rooted in the image of God:

> The differentiation of the sexes is so constitutive of humanity that, first, it appears as a primeval order (Gen. 1:27; 2:18ff.) and endures as a constant despite its depravation in the Fall (Gen. 3:16), and, second, that it is attributed symbolic value for the fundamental structure of all human existence, that is to say, for the existence of man in his relationship to his fellow man, for the fact that he is defined by his being as a Thou in relation to a Thou.[36]

Therefore, persons exist as male to female. This means that, "in affirming our own sex, we should accept and affirm the other sex as essential to our own."[37]

The shared humanity model attempts to ground personhood in the context of sexuality. One important result of this view is an emphasis upon fellowship. The male exists for the female and vice versa; both exist for God. Here the emphasis is not upon sexual intercourse but upon the way in which we exist concretely for one another. It argues against the view that the only way for a man and a woman to relate to one another is physical intimacy. It further suggests that man without woman is incomplete and vice versa.

The five models discussed in this section represent diverse perspectives. The point of discussing these issues is to suggest that sexuality is linked to personhood. Self-respect will never come until we accept our own personhood and that of others. It is lamentable that we live in a world where sexes and races compete with one another. One sure testimony to the Fall is the amount of anger and hatred in the world. Women's rights, gay rights, men's rights, and civil rights testify to the level of confrontation in our world. The list could go on, but people are set against one another on every corner. The Scripture testifies that we are called to a life of respect, for ourselves and for one another.

Self-respect is an important link in our attempt to untangle the sexual revolution. It is really a two-sided truth. First, self-respect establishes our unique relationship to God. Creation means that our origin is in God. Second, self-respect implies a real responsibility to live out the full significance of creation. This world is full of reasons to doubt that human beings are God's creation. War, violence, and the manifold inhumanity of governments and individuals are painfully apparent. Human sexuality, which was intended to mirror a person's relationship to God, has been distorted and abused. The kind of attitude that will allow a male to brag about the sexual conquest of a female diminishes the hope of self-respect. Yet the beam of light from the Judeo-Christian heritage is that our sexuality is grounded in self-respect. As we come to understand the richness of this concept, we can live healthily as sexual religious beings.

Part of what is implied by self-respect is wrapped up with love. Jesus makes it very clear that love, first, grows out of a sense of who God is, and second, out of who I am in the sight of God. Chapter 3 will examine the meaning of love as a principle for untangling the sexual revolution. Love as it grows out of self-respect is essential for dealing with our sexual existence. We will now turn to an examination of our second principle—the meaning of love.

## Summary

1. Self-respect is the biblically grounded affirmation that we are made in the image of God.

2. Humankind is called to responsibility by virtue of its unique creation.

3. Redeemed humanity bears the Holy Spirit, both as individuals and as a community, in the world. This implies that, as individuals and as a community, we are called to self-respect.

4. The Resurrection is the biblical affirmation that God is re-creating and redeeming life, thus establishing self-respect.

5. The biblical understanding of human sexuality calls us to accept it as a good gift that is central to living out the faith and the establishing of ourselves as persons.

## Notes

1. Jurgen Moltmann, *God in Creation: A New Theology of Creation and the Spirit of God* (New York: Harper and Row, Publishers, 1985), 187.

2. Claus Westermann, *Elements of Old Testament Theology*, trans. Douglas Stott (Atlanta: John Knox Press, 1982), 97.

3. Dietrich Bonhoeffer, *Creation and the Fall* (New York: Macmillan Co., 1959), 36.

4. Ibid., 37.

5. Moltmann, *God in Creation*, 219.

6. James M. Gustafson, *Ethics from a Theocentric Perspective*, vol. 1, *Theology and Ethics* (Chicago: University of Chicago Press, 1981), 50.

7. Moltmann, *God in Creation,* 188.

8. George Eldon Ladd, *A Theology of the New Testament* (Grand Rapids: William B. Eerdmans Publishing Co., 1974), 482.

9. Oliver O'Donovan, *Resurrection and Moral Order: An Outline for Evangelical Ethics* (Grand Rapids: William B. Eerdmans Publishing Co., 1986), 31.

10. Alan Richardson, *An Introduction to the Theology of the New Testament* (New York: Harper and Row, Publishers, 1958), 242.

11. Herman N. Ridderbos, *Paul: An Outline of His Theology,* trans. John Richard De Witt (Grand Rapids: William B. Eerdmans Publishing Co., 1975), 213-14.

12. Richardson, *Introduction,* 205.

13. Ladd, *Theology,* 488.

14. Paul Tillich, *The New Being* (New York: Charles Scribner's Sons, 1955), 29.

15. James B. Nelson, *Embodiment: An Approach to Sexuality and Christian Theology* (Minneapolis: Augsburg Publishing House, 1978), 272.

16. W. Norman Pittenger, *The Christian View of Sexual Behavior: A Reaction to the Kinsey Report* (Greenwich, Conn.: Seabury Press, 1954), 18.

17. Nelson, *Embodiment,* 31.

18. Ibid., 31-36.

19. Pittenger, *Christian View,* 61.

20. Augustine, *The Confessions,* trans. R. S. Pine-Coffin (New York: Penguin Books, 1961), 43.

21. Thomas Aquinas, *Summa Theologica,* trans. Fathers of the English Dominican Province (Chicago: Encyclopaedia Britannica and The Great Books, 1952), 2:749-52.

22. Pittenger, *Christian View,* 34.

23. Donald Berry, "Seeking a Theology of the Finite," *Christian Century* (Sept. 29, 1982): 953.

24. Ibid., 954.

25. Anthony Kosnik, ed., *Human Sexuality: New Directions in American Catholic Thought* (New York: Paulist Press, 1977), 82.

26. Ibid., 9.

27. Peter A. Bertocci, *Sex, Love, and the Person* (New York: Sheed and Ward, 1967), 142.

28. Lisa Sowle Cahill, *Between the Sexes: Foundations for a Christian Ethics of Sexuality* (Philadelphia: Fortress Press, 1985), 2.

29. Lewis B. Smedes, *Sex for Christians: The Limits and Liberties of Sexual Living* (Grand Rapids: William B. Eerdmans Publishing Co., 1976), 19.

30. Simone de Beauvoir, "An Androgynous World," in *Masculine/Feminine: Readings in Sexual Mythology and the Liberation of Women,* ed. Betty Roszak and Theodore Roszak (New York: Harper Colophone Books, 1969), 157.

31. Paul K. Jewett, *Man as Male and Female: A Study in Sexual Relationships for a Theological Point of View* (Grand Rapids: William B. Eerdmans Publishing Co., 1975), 61-68.

32. Barbara Ehrenreich and Deirdre English, *For Her Own Good* (Garden City, N.Y.: Anchor Press, Doubleday, 1979), 18.

33. Rosemary Radford Ruether, *New Woman—New Earth: Sexist Ideologies and Human Liberation* (New York: Seabury Press, 1975), 25.

34. Valerie Solanas, "The SCUM Manifesto," in *Masculine/Feminine* (see n. 30), 263. By the way, SCUM stands for Society for Cutting Up Men.

35. Smedes, *Sex for Christians*, 29.

36. Helmut Thielicke. *The Ethics of Sex,* trans. John W. Doberstein (New York: Harper and Row, Publishers, 1964), 3-4.

37. Jewett, *Man as Male and Female,* 49.

# 3

# The Meaning of Love

"All I ever wanted was somebody to love me!" she whispered to the nurse. Then she died. No one could understand it. The girl had everything to live for: good looks, intelligence, and friends. Yet, on that rainy day in the spring, she died in an emergency room after running out of a high school basketball game and shooting herself in the stomach.

The world, even with its self-assured face on, is searching wildly for love. Some try to find it on the streets of New York, while others contemplate suicide in San Francisco. Gangs, prostitution, and substance abuse have all been traced to the need for love and belonging. This search for love is a constant theme in much secular music. The sexual revolution was to a large extent a search for love in the midst of the meaninglessness.

Perhaps the most abused word in our culture is *love*. Given the right circumstances, one can love a hamburger, a pepperoni pizza, God, a friend, or a spouse. It should be obvious that one definition of love is not broad enough to be meaningfully applied to all these categories. Society has sufficiently cheapened the word so that it can mean almost anything, from mild attraction to the intention to seek the other's good. The purpose of this chapter is to recover a biblical understanding of love.

Sexual freedom seemed to many the opportunity to express true love. Alienation and estrangement led some to reach out for the closest person, and what often resulted was a strictly physical experience. The image of a man and woman waking up after a sexual encounter without knowing the other's name is tragic. This mentality indicates a confusion about the meaning of love.

The Scripture is one long narrative with one short but profound message—redeeming and transforming love. This begins with the affirmation of God's love but is fully realized in our call to love others. The richest possible meaning of love is indicated by its transforming power: "Only when Christianity does transvalue all values, only when the Christian understanding of human possibility is radical self-overcoming, a gift from a gracious God, does the real Christian vision of what it means to be human begin."[1] Our world is hungry for love, and it is our responsibility to share the message of transforming love. The next section will look at many of the images of love present in the Scripture.

## Biblical Images of Love

The Scripture is a book with many faces. The message contained therein is at some points so simple that one just beginning to read can understand it. Yet the Scripture also contains mysteries that challenge the most mature minds. One of its most consistent messages is love. Mark 10:13-16 tells the simple story of how Jesus called the children to His side, even though the disciples thought He was too busy. Every child who hears this story can grasp its meaning: "Jesus loves me! this I know, / For the Bible tells me so." As an adult, however, this simple story has gained depth through the years. Most of the Scripture is characterized by this multidimensional quality. These are the different faces of love.

**Covenant.** At the most basic level the message of the Scripture is that God has sought a relationship with people. The covenant with Moses and Israel testifies to His love: "Then God said, 'Behold, I am going to make a covenant. Before all your people I will perform miracles which have not been produced in all the earth . . . the people among whom you live will see the working of the Lord'" (Exod. 34:10, NASB). God through His grace has loved and established these people. This says more about God than it does about the Israelites: "He will not fail you nor destroy you nor forget the covenant with your fathers which he swore to them" (Deut. 4:31, NASB). A proper understanding of covenant will include reflection upon the faithfulness of God.

The central message of the covenant is that God has sought a loving relationship with humankind. Relationship, life-style, fidelity, and grace are all wrapped up in a full understanding of the covenant. These ideas have both theological and moral significance. In the words of Lev. 20:24, "I am the Lord your God, who has set you apart from the nations." This affirmation is part of the Holiness Code. One purpose of this code is that the people called by God will live before others like they have been called. Love implies moral responsibility.

**Ruth.** One of the best-known stories in the Old Testament is contained in the Book of Ruth. At one level this is the story of love between a mother-in-law and a daughter-in-law. At another level, it is the triumph over national and religious prejudice. Elimelech, Naomi's husband, moved to Moab because of a famine. While there he died, leaving his wife and two sons in a foreign land. Both of his sons married Moabite women (Orpah and Ruth). After 10 years both sons had died. This left Naomi with her two daughters-in-law, and she decided to return to Judah. At this point she told them, "Go back, each of you, to your mother's home" (1:8). Eventually Orpah did return, but Ruth said, "Don't urge me to leave you or to turn back from you. Where you go I will go, and where you stay I will stay. Your people will be my people and your God my God" (v. 16). According to Charles Wilson: "More than natural affection motivated Ruth. Not only was she resolute in her purpose of giving selfless devotion to a grief-stricken and bitter mother-in-law, but she was also determined to join Naomi's people in worshiping the true God."[2] The amazing thing is that this Moabite ends up in the genealogy of King David, thus Jesus.

The message of Ruth is that love is inclusive. This means that a relationship between two people can exist when the reason for it is over. Ruth did not originally choose to love Naomi; it was because of a marriage that the relationship existed at all. Yet, after Ruth's husband dies, she intends to love and care for her mother-in-law. Accordingly, "The passage is marked by a gentle insistence, a quiet resolve, and a determined discernment that reveal Ruth comprehended both the loneliness of Naomi and her own duty to stand by her mother-in-law."[3] The other theme is the triumph over national or religious prejudice. In order for love to be fully understood, we should hear the word of Paul, "For we were all baptized by one Spirit into one body—whether Jews or Greeks, slave or free" (1 Cor. 12:13). Even the barriers between Moab and Israel could not stand up to a God-nurtured love. The friendship of Ruth and Naomi stands above the prejudice of nation or religion.

**Song of Songs.** There is much disagreement on just how to interpret this little book. Theophile Meek says, "The theme of the Book is love: pure, sensuous, youthful, passionate love; love that is 'hungry as the sea.'"[4] He says further, "It is a poem in praise of love. It is expressed in romantic and radiant language. It is love poetry, folk poetry telling in passionate language of the devotion of a man and a maid."[5] While the presence of this kind of book in the canon may be startling, it should be embraced. One of the clear messages of this book is that physical love is intended by God for human beings. The words of the scripture are plain: "Let him kiss me with the kisses of his mouth—for your love is more delightful than wine" (1:2). The words of 2:2 are equally expressive: "Like a lily among thorns is my darling among the maidens." While many interpretations do exist for this book, one thing is certain: Physical, even sensuous, love is in the plan of God for humanity.

During my first pastorate a man asked me why so few sermons were preached on this little book. My first reaction? "Read it and find out!" Then it occurred to me that this book is a part of the canon for a reason. My mind has returned to this incident again and again. Why are there so few sermons on Song of Songs? Could it be that we are all a little embarrassed by its straightforward treatment of sexual love? For one reason or another most people get nervous at the mention of sexuality. It somehow does not seem consistent with our "holy faith." Perhaps the most profound message of this little book is that love can be physical and spiritual at the same time. The attempt to desexualize our faith runs counter to the message of the Scripture.

**Hosea.** This eighth-century prophet tells one of the most intriguing stories of the Old Testament. Hos. 1:2 says, "When the Lord began to speak through Hosea, the Lord said to him, 'Go, take to yourself an adulterous wife and children of unfaithfulness.'" Hosea's wife, Gomer, runs away with her lover after having had three children. Hosea is told to "go, show your love to your wife again, though she is loved by another and is an adulteress" (3:1). Therefore, the picture presented is of a man who marries a woman who commits adultery. Instead of putting her away, he is told to seek reconciliation. This is at one level a very human story, but at another it describes God's relationship to Israel. Hos. 11:1-4 speaks very insightfully concerning love:

> When Israel was a child, I loved him, and out of Egypt I called my son. But the more I called Israel, the further they went from me. They sacrificed to the Baals and they burned incense to images. It was I who taught Ephraim to walk, taking them by the arms; but they did not realize it was I who healed them. I led them with cords of human kindness, with ties of love; I lifted the yoke from their neck and bent down to feed them.

Love is a relationship that implies both joy and pain.

Hosea summoned "the people back to the only true basis of community, the early Yahwistic triad of worship, righteousness, and compassion!"[6] We have already treated covenant as a clear call to a relationship with God. The parallel theme is that those whom God loves are called to a higher life. Much of the Old Testament is really a reflection on the meaning of this relationship to which Israel has been called. The prophets attempted to remind Israel of the privileges and the responsibilities of this relationship. The message of the prophets can be summarized as follows:

1. *Spiritual Perception,* the consciousness of God, which includes awareness, discernment, and responsiveness.

2. *Moral Sensitivity,* markedly social in its reference.
3. *Knowledge of God Through Personal Relationship to Him,* a meeting of the wills, a knowing, a being known.[7]

Hosea attempts to balance the unfailing love of God with His justice. The result is as Scott describes it, "a quality of behavior among men which expresses obedience to God."[8]

**The Good Samaritan (Luke 10:25-37).** This parable is occasioned by a question: "What must I do to inherit eternal life?" (v. 25). The answer comes from the law: "'Love the Lord your God with all your heart and with all your soul and with all your strength and with all your mind' and 'Love your neighbor as yourself'" (v. 27). The simplicity of the response is only understood when one pauses to reflect upon the complexity of the law. Still, the expert in the law tries to avoid the simple truth by asking, "And who is my neighbor?" (v. 29). One understands love more clearly through action than through words. The church is called to model this love for the world: "It is of the very nature of the community of faith, therefore, that its purpose is not exhausted in its providing for the needs of its members, but extends outward to a self-transcending calling to be present wherever there is loneliness, sickness, hunger, or injustice."[9] This question is answered with a parable about a Samaritan who rendered aid to an injured man. This story is made even more pointed because both a priest and a Levite had "passed on the other side" (v. 31). The religious men had failed to be neighbors, while one who stood on the outside responded:

> It is Christ, the one who is stripped and beaten and left half dead, that the Samaritan succoured and took care of. This is the heart of Christian agape: "ye did it unto me." There is no merit in our service, for our best is unworthy of him who did so much for us. The poor sufferer when I help confers a favor on me, not I on him, because he shews me Christ, makes Christ real to me, enables me to touch, handle, tend, and serve Christ.[10]

A godly love always reaches out. The mystery, however, is that as we love our neighbor, Christ is revealed. Love often becomes a path toward facing real human hurt. Religion easily gets wrapped up in words. The law can debate the details of procedure so fully that it misses the big picture. A love that stops to render aid is grounded in God, not religion or law. If love means anything at all, it means that we reach out to those who need us. The promise of Scripture is that as we do this, we do it unto Christ. The question is not Who is my neighbor? but Am I a person who really loves?

**The Lost Sheep (Luke 15:1-7).** William Barclay refers to this parable when he says, "There is a wondrous thought here. It is the truly tremendous truth that God is kinder than men."[11] All of the Gospels make the point that Jesus preferred the company of those who were seeking God. Whether these people were associated with the religious group did not seem to matter. The Pharisees frequently complained that Jesus "welcomes sinners and eats with them" (v. 2). The parable of the lost sheep arises out of this very problem in the minds of the Pharisees. The story describes the joy of the shepherd who carefully put the lost sheep on his shoulders and carries it to safety. This means that "the shepherd considers no trouble, sacrifice and suffering too great to find the lost sheep and bring it back."[12]

Love always seeks the other; it is never content to wait with folded arms. "In no other religion in the whole world does one come to know God as the One who in His love seeks the lost person to save him through His grace. In the writings of the other religions we see how man seeks and yearns for God, but in the Bible we see how God in Christ seeks man to save him for time and eternity."[13] As God reaches out for us, we are called to reach out to others. This motivates us to evangelism for the whole person. It also implies that our relationship with one another ought to be characterized by the joy and sacrifice that is typical of Christ's ministry.

**The Loving Father (Luke 15:11-32).** This is one of the best-known parables of the New Testament. It tells the story of a man who decides to collect his inheritance so that he might experience the good life. But he ends up feeding pigs and longing "to fill his stomach with the pods that the pigs were eating" (v. 16). This is a position lower than that of the hired hands on his father's farm. He decides, then, to go to his father and ask for a job. Verse 20 describes the meeting of father and son: "But while he was still a long way off, his father saw him and was filled with compassion for him; he ran to his son, threw his arms around him and kissed him." This is surely one of the great images of Christianity.

It is a mistake to focus our attention on the son who squanders "his wealth in wild living" (v. 13). For the real story concerns the father who waits for his son and immediately welcomes him back. The other side of the story relates to the stingy older brother who begrudges the renewed status of the wayward son. He would have no doubt preferred that his returning brother be sent away, or at the very best forced to work a lowly job on the farm. Instead, the father reestablishes the prodigal son to his original status.

This parable presents two images of love. One is the beautiful story of a father who accepts his wayward son back home. This love is able to forgive and reinstate the son who had sinned against his father. The other image of love is the brother who thinks of love in terms of an inheritance. His love for his brother, and perhaps his father, is based on what he can get out of them. The message of the scripture is that God loves us like the father loved the wayward son. This means that we are called away from an attitude like the unforgiving brother. Love implies forgiveness.

**First Corinthians 13.** The central theme of this chapter can be easily paraphrased: "Nowhere does love emerge more clearly than here in its character as binding together and involving the church. We have Paul's struggle against spiritual individualism in the Christian church to thank for the celebrated chapters 1 Corinthians 12 and 13."[14] Most of us are aware that Corinth was not a moral place. The Epistle reads like a catalog of everything that could be wrong with a church. Perhaps the most devastating problem was the spiritual hierarchy that overemphasized "gifts." First Corinthians stands as a sure testimony that love is the most important virtue of all. Without it we are little more than a "resounding gong or a clanging cymbal" (v. 1). This is made even clearer by the closing verse of the chapter, "But the greatest of these is love" (v. 13).

A close reading of this chapter reveals a more subtle truth: Love is a communal undertaking. Love is characterized as patient, kind, not envying, not boasting, not being proud, and so on. All of the characteristics are relational. This point can easily be lost in the rush to characterize love. Emphasis upon miracles often calls glory to the one who performs them. Speaking in tongues can lead to the impression that one has a privileged place with God. The list could go on, but Paul reminds the Corinthians that love alone will keep a church together. When love characterizes the fellowship, it makes a real difference. Love calls us together; it "always protects, always trusts, always hopes, always perseveres" (v. 7). You really cannot love a hamburger, but in the power of God's grace it is possible to love another human being.

**First John.** It can be said of this Epistle that "no other book of the Bible treats so many doctrines so concisely and so well."[15] Yet "it is not doctrine for the sake of a system of theology, but doctrine as the basis of fellowship with God and a life of perfect love."[16] My interest in looking at the book is to determine its message concerning love. John links morality and theology directly: "This is how we know who the children of God are and who the children of the devil are: Anyone who does not do what is right is not a child of God; nor is anyone who does not love his brother" (3:10). This message is further reinforced in the next verse, "We should love one another" (v. 11). John characterizes the meaning of this love by looking at the life of Christ. It is in the deeds of Christ that we see most clearly what love really means.

This little Epistle also carries the profound message that "love comes from God. Everyone who loves has been born of God and knows God" (4:7). Does this include sexual love? What does it say about the meaning of love? Perhaps part of the answer is as follows: "God is love. Whoever lives in love lives in God, and God in him. . . . love is made complete among us so that we will have confidence on the day of judgment, because in this world we are like him. . . . We love because he first loved us" (vv. 16-17, 19). The love John refers to includes sexual love. This is not to suggest that physical love is always like this, but it can be. God created us as sexual beings, and through the appropriate use of sexuality, we can participate in God's love. The kind of love we are talking about is full, human, erotic, agapeic, spiritual, and in some measure divine. One cannot love God and abuse a spouse, either physically or emotionally. We do not have license to be cruel and unresponsive to the person we love. The Epistle presents Christ's life as the paradigm for defining love. The point seems to be that Christianity is about a relationship, and the "agape about which St. John speaks is . . . obedience to the divine commandment to exhibit . . . in actual brotherly love, the very agape with which the Father loves the Son and the Son the Father."[17]

Because the Bible presents several images of love, it is helpful to examine any common themes. For a contemporary discussion on sexuality, the nine images we have shared in this section have illustrated some of the relevance of the biblical view. Each scripture talks about love in a unique way, but with common messages.

First, all love originates in God. Taken in its most serious form, this means that if love exists anywhere, then it comes from God. Whether God is named or not, when a person truly loves, he is participating in the divine gift of love. Perhaps this is most clearly seen in 1 John, but the message is heard in the other passages as well. The love between Ruth and Naomi can only exist through God. Many things may feel like love, but love is only possible through God.

Second, love fulfills the law. One of the standing battles of the Christian faith has been grace and law. The Scriptures say no real opposition exists between law and love. It might be possible to require that a person be nice to another, but love cannot be mandated. Perhaps we have come to think of love as little more than politeness, but this is wrong. Love is a strong word that means a commitment to morality. It is self-contradictory to assume that the law of God is different from the love of God.

Third, love is concrete. It is not possible to love abstractly or impersonally. Love reaches out to the beloved without prompting. It may mean stopping to render aid or looking for the lost sheep. It could mean staying with a bitter mother-in-law or enjoying the erotic love of Song of Songs. There is a sense in which love is an idea; but in a deeper sense it is a hand extended to another.

Fourth, love opens and illuminates our future. When love becomes so possessive that it seeks ownership, then it ceases to be love. It is possible to allow the other to be an individual when love characterizes the relationship. The partnership in marriage can in its highest expression lead to a unity of soul and flesh that creates a more secure future for husband and wife.

Finally, love implies self-love. This relates closely to self-respect. It won't be possible for us to love another person until we love ourselves. Only when we see ourselves as God sees us is it possible to love another. Perhaps we need to remind ourselves that God stands ready to welcome us back to the Kingdom. The other image presented in the parable of the prodigal is equally profound: "My son . . . you are always with me and everything I have is yours" (Luke 15:31). These words spoken by the father to the elder brother remind us that he loved both sons. This love should have characterized all of the relationships including the one between the brothers. The love that God establishes in us engenders a loving life-style. It is God's love that makes all loving relationships possible.

All of these are a part of what love means. A song popular in the early 1970s asserts, "What the world needs now is love, sweet love, / No, not just for some but for everyone."* This implies that love is concrete:

> Love, then, involves commitment to the other, the willingness to risk and entrust oneself to the other. It is the desire to give and to open the self in personal nakedness to the be-

loved. Along with the agapeic quality, there is also the erotic desire to receive whatever the other will give to the self. Love is expectant. It recognizes the inexhaustible possibilities in the beloved, expecting that enriching novelty and surprise will emerge from the relationship. Love is the respect of individual identity.[18]

Many definitions of love do exist, but all true love is grounded in God. Love is real, it is concrete, it seeks the other's good, and it shares out of its depth. A major concern when one talks about love is intimacy. There is even a sense in which the sexual revolution related primarily to intimacy. This means that our relationships with one another change as a result of the revolution. When we live in the world among strangers, there is neither love nor intimacy. Either without the other is a perversion, but when they converge, it is a gift of God.

## Intimacy and Love

In the previous section we defined love by using nine illustrations of love from the Bible. The emphases were diverse: relationship, friendship, eroticism, forgiveness, and so on. All of these are important for a full understanding of love. But there is one ingredient that must concern all love: intimacy. We will discuss intimacy here: friendship and marriage. There are, of course, many other types of intimacy, but these two are especially relevant as we try to fully understand the meaning of love.

**Friendship** is one clear expression of intimacy. Biblically, we can see many expressions of friendship: Jonathan and David; Ruth and Naomi; Paul and Silas; and so on. The making of friends is a fundamental task for all human beings. Strangely, in a time when more people are moving into urban centers, we are more alienated from one another than in the past. No matter how much technology has to offer, the need to find intimate communion is still necessary. Intimacy is the ability to express one's true feelings. We all have friends with whom we share simple pleasures. At another level there is the intimacy that we have with a very special friend. Still deeper is the intimacy that we have with a spouse. We share a part of ourselves in each of these cases. All of these are appropriate and helpful to our happiness. There is a sense in which this quest has a Christian dimension, for one's capacity to know God is often tied to his ability to trust on the human level.

We have all met the people who have no ability to trust other people. There is, perhaps, inside of every one of us the memory of having trusted a person only to be disappointed. When this kind of frustration begins to characterize one's entire life, it reduces his capacity to be happy. The need for friendship goes to the very soul of humankind.

Friendship is a long process. We can't wake up one morning and be intimate with another person; relationships have to be nurtured over time. Every person is involved in a personal pilgrimage. We are what we have become through the process of growth, success, failure, happiness, sadness, and dreams. Nothing in life stands alone; rather it is a part of a very complex pattern. Growing involves having relationships with other people. Friendship is not a commodity all neatly wrapped up in a package; rather it is an invitation to know another human being.

Another aspect of friendship is the willingness to take a risk and be vulnerable. This risking goes against the credo of the "Rambo generation." Such a person needs no one, and there are no tears or forgiveness. If we accept the call to relationship that lies deep within each of us, there may be hurt and even betrayal. Taking that risk may instead mean joy and fidelity. Life is only safe when it is lived away from people, or with shields and barriers all around. If we choose to withdraw in order to avoid the risk, we will not grow, neither will we love or be loved.

The fact that all relationships imply a certain measure of risk does not legitimize a reckless approach. A woman once stopped into my office to ask for prayer. She carefully explained that her marriage was not good. This was hard to understand, since she said God had told her to marry this man. Later in the conversation, she said that her husband had been married six times previous to this. God is often blamed for our reckless choices. Two other women in the church had survived a marriage to alcoholic and abusive men only to marry another man with the same problem. The fact that each of us needs intimacy so desperately can lead to foolish choices. All relationships require risk, but some are unreasonable and should be avoided. We cannot and indeed should not be seeking intimacy with everyone we meet. Yet one bad experience should not be an excuse for never trusting another person. Life should teach us how to balance judgment with transparency.

The meaning of intimacy in the context of relationship is the ability to make and honor commitments at a number of levels. Understanding the appropriate boundaries of intimacy is essential. There is a level of intimacy that is reserved for my wife. It would be inappropriate for me to seek marital intimacy with another person. Yet, friendship implies intimacy, and it is appropriate to share a part of oneself with a friend. All of these commitments must have a center, and for Christians this ought to be God, who is able to keep relationships in balance. Because intimacy operates at a number of levels, one can be married and still have other friends. In fact, a marriage that is characterized by jealousy of all other contact is weak. While the deepest and most profound level of intimacy is marriage, many other meaningful relationships can be maintained.

We are now in a time when all too many relationships between people are sexualized. I once had a student tell me that he believed the only place a close relationship existed between a man and woman is the bedroom. We should hear the words of Lewis Smedes: "The more we believe that all sexual relationships have only the bed as their terminus, the more people involved in sexual relationships will act on that premise."[19] There is a sense in which all relationships are sexual, but this does not imply sexual intercourse. The fact that we are sexual does not mean that every relationship must be sexualized.

It is important that we distinguish between sexual and sexualized relationships. Every person is born either male or female. This implies a great deal about the kind of person we are, how we will relate to others. I am a male, and this describes the way that I am in the world. Because I am a male does not mean that crying after an episode of "Highway to Heaven" is not appropriate. It does not mean that I should be paid more for doing the same job as a female colleague. One's sexuality cannot be separated from the way one relates to other people. All relationships are sexual in a fundamental way. It is one thing to say that one relates sexually; it is quite another to suggest that a relationship is sexualized. One sexualizes a relationship by reducing its value to intercourse: "People also tend to confuse the physical desire for sex with the affective desire for intimacy. We experience sexual desire and think that what we need is genital satisfaction when actually we are longing for closeness."[20] It is a dangerous attitude that sexualizes all relationships with the opposite sex. While it is foolish to deny the reality of the strong physical attraction between people of the opposite sex, it is not necessary for all male-female relationships to be sexualized.

Friendship constitutes real commitment to another person. It is a gift that two people choose to give one another. It also represents a willingness to be honest with one another. Everybody needs somebody to be honest with them, perhaps several people. This means a willingness to gently direct or persuade a person of the truth, even when it is easier to let them believe a lie. Friendship includes forgiveness. It is impossible to care for another person and not be offended by the person at least occasionally. A person who does not learn to forgive will be unhappy. Finally, friendship exists in the life of grace. There is a great deal of sinful separation in our world today that can be overcome in Christian friendship. It is possible to experience God's grace through human relationships. We have the privilege of forming a community of faith where people are respected not by secular standards but by the fact that we are Christian. This is only possible in the life of grace.

Somewhere between friendship and marriage the question of sexuality must be addressed. The thread that links friendship and marriage is intimacy, and it is tied to our sexuality. This is because "sexuality is a sign, a symbol, and a means of our call to communication and communion."[21]

Probably the first time any of us struggled with sin, it was related to our quest for sexual identity. During that painful, yet hopeful, period known as puberty, the real need is for intimacy and acceptance. I remember very well the agony of this period in my life. During the ninth grade something happened that still seems real. Every school has its physically attractive crowd; these people are the elite. I was much closer to the "nerd" faction than to the "elites." One particular girl was the most attractive of all. Her name was Norma Jean, and the mere mention of her name was enough to excite half the school. Miracle of miracles, she sat in front of me in algebra class. She never spoke to me, but there she sat. One day in the spring, however, she did turn to me and ask me to scratch her back. I can still remember Eddie's voice from the back of the classroom: "Go for it!" I didn't comply, but this incident has always illustrated for me the "painful-yet-joyous region" that sexuality represents. This region lies somewhere between desire and judgment.

The quest for intimacy is especially difficult when the opposite sex is involved. At this point two things need to be said. First, it is necessary that we learn how to relate to the opposite sex as persons instead of sexual objects. An individual is something more than the sum of body parts. Second, it is essential that we learn how to be intimate with the person we marry: "A sexual act may or may not be procreative, but it is always an avenue of personal communication, and a constituent of the most intense and intimate human relationship possible."[22] Marriage will be addressed more fully later in the chapter, but there is no doubt that the highest form of intimacy is the marriage covenant.

Part of what it means to be human is the ability to relate to the opposite sex without sexualizing the relationship. A person of the opposite sex is just that, a person. While it is not possible, or advisable, that we forget the sexuality of the other person, it is not necessary to sexualize the relationship. It is possible for persons of the opposite sex to have solid, growing, and fulfilling relationships. The women's movement is forcing us to see what should have been all too apparent. Women have the same dreams and needs as their male counterparts. There is nothing in the Scripture that requires a woman to be subhuman, to be the property of a male-dominated society. We relate best as people who are free to love in the context of mutual respect.

Friendship is an important dimension of intimacy. It should be possible for men and women to be friends without stepping over the boundaries of marriage. As we have already observed, the cultural forces apparent in the 20th century have fostered alienation and estrangement. Ours is a time of enhanced public communication, but often at the expense of personal communication. On the sexual level this mentality reduces people to objects. But love is more than a genital phenomenon, it is a call to participate with others in the making of a better world. The ability to make and honor commitments to one another is essential to our happiness.

**Marriage** "is a crucible into which two persons let themselves be thrown."[23] It can also be called a covenant of agape.[24] According to Smedes, "The physical intimacy, the abandonment in trust, the unique closeness—all these things hint at and become a sign of a deep personal union sealed between two people by physical union."[25] The tombstone for marriage has been carved many times, but it has survived. A recent survey estimated that 6 million divorced people live in the United States. The tragedy of divorce has struck almost every family, or so it seems. Yet, when one has an intimate and growing marriage, it is a beautiful thing. Such a marriage defies analysis, because it mirrors the love of Christ for His Church (Eph. 5:21-33). A good marriage can combine all the characteristics of friendship with the added dimension brought by sexual intercourse. The importance of marriage needs to be emphasized: "A biblical theology of sexuality is equivalent to a theology of marriage. To celebrate sex is to celebrate the totality of marriage; to celebrate marriage is to celebrate the totality of sex."[26]

Marriage is first and most importantly a covenant of love. It is characterized by a participation in one another's life. It is more than Luther suspected it could be when he referred to it as an "emergency hospital of human drives."[27] It is even more than Paul suggests, "It is good for them to stay unmarried, as I am. But if they cannot control themselves, they should marry, for it is better to marry than to burn with passion" (1 Cor. 7:8-9). It is, perhaps, better described by Small: "When a man and a woman unite in marriage, humanity experiences a restoration to wholeness."[28] Another image of marriage is captured in the following: "When a man and a woman who have lived together, or, on the night of their marriage, intend, with all their hearts and souls, to live together in faithful mutuality, with tenderness one for the other, with patience and helpfulness one towards the other, enter upon that experience of physical love which culminates in their actual union through their sexual organs the act is no isolated thing."[29] This means that marriage is multidimensional, as it allows two people to love and participate in one another.

The sexual revolution has changed many things, including marriage. Statistics seem to suggest that more people are choosing to live together, thereby minimizing the risk of a lifetime commitment. Because of hurt and fear many people find it difficult to make a commitment to another person. Even without the ring and the certificate, people find that living together is not risk free. A sizable percentage of those who marry after having lived together end up divorced. The fact that people are still getting married should indicate that deep within, people know nothing is quite so fulfilling as a good marriage.

It is in the context of marriage that God intends sexual intercourse. The parameters of sexual intercourse are easy to determine according to the Scripture: marriage. "When intercourse takes place in a loving marriage it has several qualities and results: it expresses gratitude to God for creation; it means a communication more powerful than speech; through it the couple come to understand the meaning of masculinity and femininity; and intercourse is always an accurate reflection of the whole relationship which the couple has."[30] Sexual intercourse really cannot be separated from the context of marriage and have much meaning at all. There is adequate testimony to the fact that sexuality is abused. The person who uses his sexuality to get something is abusing God's good gift. A person who degrades his spouse and then has sexual intercourse is abusing a God-given privilege. The list could go on, but the point is that the God-blessed ability to so clearly mesh with another person should be cherished.

Marriage is much more than a fence built around two people. What it can be is an invitation to experience more fully what God intended people to be. In 1973 I married a beautiful young woman. The vows we said to one another in the presence of God were real; they were a testimony to our intentions. Yet, "to love, honor, and cherish" only partially describes our relationship now. God has blessed our home with many things including three lovely children. No human being understands me better than my wife. We have laughed and cried together. We have been angry and misunderstood one another, but these quickly recede in the light of the joy and understanding we have known together. Marriage is not a concept, it is a relationship with a woman who chooses to love me and whom I choose to love. This is not to suggest that our life together is perfect when judged against some artificial or absolute standard. It is not to suggest that the way we have come to relate together is the only possible way a marriage should go. It is to suggest that marriage can be a path to fulfillment.

It is not possible to fully treat marriage without some mention of divorce. Certainly, the dark human agony represented in any divorce is tragic. The sexual revolution has had the effect of loosening the taboos related to divorce. Most Christians even 40 years ago would have been against divorce in almost every case. Today, even in the evangelical church there is a tendency to add to the already long list of acceptable reasons for obtaining divorce.

The biblical case for divorce is well known. Basically, divorce is permissible in the case of infidelity. Mark 10:1-12 is the classical passage concerning divorce. The words of Jesus are plain: "Anyone who divorces his wife and marries another woman commits adultery against her. And if she divorces her husband and marries another man, she commits adultery" (vv. 11-12). There can be very little doubt that

Christian tradition has felt that marriage is God's plan for humankind's sexual fulfillment. It is equally true that divorce is understood as the disruption of this plan for humanity. Recent studies have shown that no single thing is quite so painful for a child as living through the divorce of parents. As Christians we must do everything within our power to contribute positively to the family life. The Christian tradition stands for marriage and against divorce.

Having said all the above concerning marriage, it must be acknowledged that we do not live in a perfect world. Most of the choices that we need to make will be difficult. I have counseled with women who were battered and otherwise abused by their husbands. One particular case comes to mind of a woman who had been nearly beaten to death by her husband. When I first met her, she was recovering from a suicide attempt in an intensive care unit. I do not believe that it was my responsibility to tell her to return to that man. Divorce is ugly, but there are circumstances where it is advisable and moral. We in the church are called to take up the case of the oppressed, and many times this includes the woman who is fleeing from her husband. I cannot imagine that Jesus would ask a woman who has been abused or who has watched her children be abused to stay in that kind of marriage. Whatever the Scripture teaches about divorce, it does not condone situations of manifold pain.

The answer to the problem of divorce is not to condemn it in all cases but to strengthen the foundation for marriage. In our less-than-perfect world divorce is sometimes necessary. By standing for marriage, we declare that divorce is a serious problem. It should be understood as a tragedy on a number of levels: husband, wife, and children. But the real issue is intimacy, fidelity, and responsibility. I am calling for a renewed effort in the church to honor marriage. This is the note sounded in the Scripture.

The last decade has made it possible for men and women to more fully express their feelings. Men have felt a freedom to be vulnerable during the last several years. During this same period of time the femininity of women has not been questioned by the pursuit of a career. These two statements, while a bit idealistic, are also true in some measure. Overcoming the sinful separation that often characterizes our world will require a definition of love that includes intimacy. Our teens should be affirmed by love in the church and especially in the home. Sexual intercourse is not the prize for acceptance, it is the union of two souls within the context of marriage. True love is not found in the backseat of an automobile, it is the process of mutuality and respect. The meaning of love is most fully expressed in the fact that "while we were yet sinners, Christ died for us" (Rom. 5:8, KJV). This should remind us that love always gives more than it takes, and it leaves a person more free than before. This kind of relationship cannot be legislated. It can only arise out of a heart of love.

We have dealt with two principles for untangling the sexual revolution: self-respect and the meaning of love. Together they present an image of the difference that God's grace makes for our sexual existence. They help us to answer two questions: Who am I? and What should characterize our relationships? When these issues are understood in light of the gospel, it is possible to deal creatively with the tensions and possibilities created by the sexual revolution. The next chapter will deal with the final principle, responsible freedom. After we have answered the questions that are suggested above, it is necessary to take another step. It is important that we look at the resources of law and grace for a solid understanding of our sexual responsibilities. We will now turn to this task.

## Summary

1. Love is a multidimensional reality that encompasses family relationships, friends, spouse, and many other types of relationships.

2. The Scripture gives us insight into love through its depiction of its diverse expressions: relationship, friendship, erotic love, forgiveness, patience, and communality.

3. Intimacy is the thread that links all the expressions of love. It can be defined as the ability to be real with some people all the time and with all people some of the time.

4. Friendship is the commitment to be intimate at an appropriate level with another human being.

5. Marriage is the ultimate expression of intimacy on the human level; it mirrors the love of God for creation.

6. An understanding of love is essential to untangling the sexual revolution.

## Notes

1. David Tracy, "Christian Faith and Radical Equality," *Theology Today* 34 (January 1978): 370.

2. Charles Wilson, "The Book of Ruth," in *The Wesleyan Bible Commentary,* vol. 1, pt. 2 (Grand Rapids: William B. Eerdmans Publishing Co., 1967), 125.

3. James Cleland, "The Book of Ruth—Exposition," in *The Interpreter's Bible,* vol. 2 (Nashville: Abingdon Press, 1956), 834.

4. Theophile Meek, "Song of Songs—Introduction and Exegesis," in *The Interpreter's Bible,* vol. 5 (Nashville: Abingdon Press, 1956), 98.

5. Ibid.

6. Paul Hanson, *The People Called: The Growth of Community in the Bible* (New York: Harper and Row, Publishers, 1986), 166.

7. R. B. Y. Scott, *The Relevance of the Prophets* (New York: Macmillan Co., 1944, 1968), 210-13.

8. Ibid., 214.

9. Hanson, *People Called,* 503.

10. Richardson, *Introduction,* 137.

11. William Barclay, "The Gospel of Luke," in *The Daily Study Bible* (Philadelphia: Westminster Press, 1953, 1956), 208.

12. Norval Geldenhuys, "Commentary on the Gospel of Luke," in *The New International Commentary of the New Testament* (Grand Rapids: William B. Eerdmans Publishing Co., 1951), 402.

13. Ibid., 403.

14. Ridderbos, *Paul,* 295.

15. Harvey J. S. Blaney, "The First Epistle of John," in *Beacon Bible Commentary,* vol. 10 (Kansas City: Beacon Hill Press of Kansas City, 1967), 343.

16. Ibid.

17. Richardson, *Introduction,* 287.

18. Nelson, *Embodiment,* 117.

19. Smedes, *Sex for Christians,* 153.

20. Gennaro P. Avvento, *Sexuality: A Christian View* (Mystic, Conn.: Twenty-third Publications, 1982), 13.

21. Nelson, *Embodiment*, 18.

22. Cahill, *Between the Sexes*, 141.

23. Bertocci, *Sex, Love, and the Person*, 16.

24. Nelson, *Embodiment*, 133.

25. Smedes, *Sex for Christians*, 134.

26. Dwight Small, *Christian: Celebrate Your Sexuality* (Old Tappan, N.J.: Fleming H. Revell Co., 1974), 205.

27. Nelson, *Embodiment*, 55.

28. Small, *Christian: Celebrate*, 144.

29. Pittenger, *Christian View*, 35-36.

30. Nelson, *Embodiment*, 137.

# 4

# Responsible Freedom

My first summer job was working in the mail room of a large office building. I was 16 years old and naive about life. Because of my youth the older guys in the mail room took it upon themselves to "educate" me concerning sex. This was the summer of 1968, and the rhetoric of sexual freedom ran high. In many ways that summer was very painful. Since I was raised in a Christian home, the attitude expressed by these people was foreign to me.

I remember a particular day when one of my coworkers seemed preoccupied. About midmorning Joe informed the rest of us that a girl he dated was pregnant. It was almost funny to me that this "macho man" would be in such a predicament. (I was too young to see beyond him to the girl who would ultimately have to deal with the problem.) Joe firmly told us he had no intention of marrying this girl. All he ever did, he said, was park with her on some dark country road. He didn't even know her!

As it turned out, the girl was not pregnant. But it has always seemed important to me that her plight did not really matter to him. His sexual liberation had led to her sexual bondage. Eventually this so-called sexual liberation would lead to his own bondage. Whether to appetite or to disease, those who pursue sexual liberation as Joe did always surrender their freedom. But the promise of the Scripture is that the children of God can have real freedom. This freedom is never at the expense of others. Real liberation frees us to be what God intended.

We have addressed two fundamental principles for dealing with the sexual revolution. The first principle is self-respect. All decisions concerning sexual behavior should arise out of who God intended us to be. The second principle is the centrality of love. Only when we understand that love comes from God and is meant to reach our neighbor will our sexual behavior reflect our Creator. These two principles demand that we understand who we are and how our relationships should be shaped. They, at least in some measure, help us set the parameters of our sexual behavior. The purpose of this chapter is to explore a third principle: responsible freedom. The nature of Christian freedom is only fully understood in the context of responsibility. Freedom grows out of an understanding of grace; responsibility is linked to the law in the same way. This helps us to understand the relationship between theology and ethics.

## The Parameters of the Christian Life

The Scripture has a great deal to say about the Christian life. The attempt to define exactly what it means to be a Christian is a consistent theological theme. Two concepts have usually defined the parameters of the Christian life: grace and law. The middle ground between "lawless grace" and "graceless law" is where Christianity is lived. A "lawless grace" attempts to sanctify any action by this rationale: "God understands that I am only human." The plain fact is that the gospel calls us to moral living. At the other extreme is "graceless law," which regards almost everything as evil. Rules, restrictions, and standards become more important than people. This is the attitude of the Pharisees, who followed Jesus so that each infraction of the law might be recorded. The balance between the extremes of "lawless grace" and "graceless law" is responsible freedom. Perhaps it will be easier to understand this middle ground if we look carefully at both grace and law.

**Grace** is central to any adequate understanding of the gospel. In the New Testament the basic understanding of grace is free giving. Accordingly, it is "not just a quality of God but its actualization at the cross (Gal. 2:21) and its proclamation in the gospel."[1] The correct understanding of grace is tied to the Christ event. This makes the Christian message with its attending moral imperative good news. It means the essential message of the gospel is that God loves us and calls us to love others. This joyful proclamation grows out of the Old Testament. Ps. 5:11 reads, "But let all who take refuge in you be glad; let them ever sing for joy. Spread your protection over them, that those who love your name may rejoice in you." This idea is further expressed in 16:11, "You have made known to me the path of life; you will fill me with joy in your presence, with eternal pleasures at your right hand." We can fully understand the richness of this idea only in the context of redemption.

As grace is developed in the Old Testament, it "denotes a gracious disposition that finds expression in a gracious action."[2] The term is most often used when a person calls upon God to hear prayer, to heal, to redeem, to pardon, and to strengthen.[3] Therefore, grace in the Old Testament comes to mean an activity of God toward humankind: healing, pardoning, and so on. It means that God has related himself to His people, to all people: "I will betroth you to me forever; I will betroth you in righteousness and justice, in love and compassion. I will betroth you in faithfulness, and you will acknowledge the Lord" (Hos. 2:19-20). Because God has so freely related himself to humankind, we are to be compassionate as well. His faithfulness and love should characterize all our relationships. Our morality should be established upon this foundation of God's gracious activity toward us.

One of the more interesting explications of grace is found in Col. 3:12—4:1. These verses define our relationship with God: "chosen people, holy and dearly loved" (3:12). This thought forms the entire fabric of the Christian life: We are loved. Several years ago after having preached a sermon on the love of God, I met a young woman at the rear of the church. She was very polite, but there was a sadness that seemed to cloud her countenance. After talking awhile, she opened up a bit about some of her frustrations and failures.

Finally I asked her if she believed that God loved her. "No!" she said. There was not a long explanation, just loneliness and desperation. Two weeks later she committed suicide.

Grace extends to every person. It comes down to real people, people with names and addresses. Love and grace have no meaning apart from relationship. Colossians makes this clear when it talks about grace: compassion, kindness, humility, gentleness, patience, forgiveness, and love. They are relational words, and they have relevance for family, church, work, and school. A world in need of love shouldn't hear a message from the Church laced with hate and condemnation. Christians are called to mirror the love of God for people.

The supreme example of grace is revealed in Jesus Christ: "For God so loved the world that he gave his one and only Son, that whoever believes in him shall not perish but have eternal life" (John 3:16). Theologians William Greathouse and H. Ray Dunning explain it this way:

> Our salvation is by divine grace, not by human endeavor. This means two things: First, our salvation is by God's gracious provision in the cross of Jesus. This is "objective" grace, sometimes defined as God's unmerited favor in Christ. Second, our salvation is by God's gracious assistance through the Holy Spirit. This may be termed "subjective" grace: God at work within our hearts awakening, convicting, converting, cleansing us.[4]

Grace and love are really two sides of one truth. In fact, "Agape-love is rightly described as 'the center of Christianity,' the Christian fundamental motif par excellence."[5] The cross of Christ is the point at which grace and love are perfectly intertwined. Ephesians instructs us: "Be imitators of God, therefore, as dearly loved children and live a life of love, just as Christ loved us and gave himself up for us as a fragrant offering and sacrifice to God" (5:1-2).

Moral responsibility arises out of a clear understanding of love and grace. Rom. 13:10 says, "Love does no harm to its neighbor." First John 5:3 adds, "This is love for God: to obey his commands. And his commands are not burdensome." Love is commitment that works itself out into the various relationships of life. The essence of responsibility is to see the imperative of the gospel. This suggests the need "to show how religious faith and belief are claimed to affect moral dispositions, attitudes, and intentions, and to indicate how a moral imperative to love is inferred from a religious belief."[6] Love is not merely a warm, fuzzy feeling, it is a dogged commitment to be moral.

The love that arises out of grace is a principle of life. Gal. 5:22-23 describes it: "But the fruit of the Spirit is love, joy, peace, patience, kindness, goodness, faithfulness, gentleness and self-control. Against such things there is no law." We are not given patience or kindness, they arise out of *agapē*. Mildred Wynkoop explains this concept further:

> *Agape,* however, is a completely different dimension of love. It is a quality of a person rather than a different kind of love. It is a principle by which one orders life—or by which life is ordered. Out of it all the relationships of life derive their character. It is not a new, infused ability but a personal orientation reaching first to God and then, by necessity, to all other persons and things in life. . . . It is not first of all an emotion but a deliberate policy whereby the relations sustained with other persons are kept in balance by one's deliberate orientation to God.[7]

Agape love grows out of God and extends toward one's neighbor.

All of this has significant implications. First, love is for the whole person. Where the sexual revolution is concerned, it will not be enough to talk about ideas. We must look to real, living, feeling, and loving persons. Second, love moves one beyond admiration to dedication. Too often talk about love and grace stops at the emotional dimension. When this happens, any moral significance is lost.

We have seen that grace is an essential ingredient to a clear understanding of Christian ethics. But reflection upon issues relating to the Christian life have consistently radiated between grace and law. Now let's look at the other side of the equation.

**Law** and its interpretation is woven throughout the fabric of the Old Testament. There is a real sense in which it gives love a structure. The seriousness attached to observing the law is clear in the Old Testament: "Whoever does not obey the law of God and the law of the king must surely be punished by death, banishment, confiscation of property, or imprisonment" (Ezra 7:26). There are many shades of meaning in the Old Testament for law, but "the most frequent and characteristic Old Testament word translated 'law' is the Hebrew *torah,* which originally signified authoritative instruction."[8]

Much of the history of Israel can be written by looking at the way the people regarded the law. During the eighth century B.C. the nation Israel tended to ignore the law altogether. The Israelites took advantage of the poor, accepted Baal worship, and acted dishonestly in business. The incidence of male and female prostitution, sometimes in conjunction with Temple worship, all indicated the dissolution of the law. It is in this context that Amos, the prophet of God's justice, steps forward. Amos speaks clearly: "Hear this word, you cows of Bashan on Mount Samaria, you women who oppress the poor and crush the needy" (4:1). Again he speaks: "You turn justice into bitterness and cast righteousness to the ground" (5:7). Amos levels another charge: "You trample on the poor and force him to give you grain. Therefore, though you have built stone mansions, you will not live in them; though you have planted lush vineyards, you will not drink their wine" (v. 11). Amos reminds Israel as well as Christians of the importance of the law. Whenever the law is obeyed, the people are blessed. When the law is disregarded, the people suffer the consequences. Whenever there is a spiritual revival, it is accompanied by a renewed interest in the law.

What is true of ancient Israel is also true of New Testament Palestine. C. M. Horne says, "Jesus not only condemned the wrong use of the law. He also confirmed its validity and pointed to its right use."[9] Both in the early Christian community and in the writings of Paul there is a deep reverence for the Mosaic law. All this indicates that the law is part of vital Christianity. The attitude toward it has generally been one of obedience or at least respect. Let's explore some of the many dimensions of the law in the Scripture.

First, there is the implication of the "letter of the law."

Exod. 30:21 says, "This is to be a lasting ordinance for Aaron and his descendants for the generations to come." The clear emphasis here is upon the exact prescription of the law. W. A. Whitehouse defines it in this way: "By 'law' we mean judicial rules of evaluation, which have binding force, and which give expression to the idea of law in those relationships of human community life which are common concern."[10] There is a real significance attached here to the exact laws and what they prescribe. John 19:7 illustrates the letter of the law: "The Jews insisted, 'We have a law, and according to that law he must die, because he claimed to be the Son of God.'" Here the religious authorities have caught the letter of the law and are doing evil because of it. In the best sense of the word, law cannot be understood in terms of the "letter." To do so perverts its true meaning.

Second, the law is a part of our heritage. We are to remember it (Mal. 4:4). The law is tangible, therefore we can be accountable to obey it. The law becomes a testimony of the entire community of faith. It is a visible way to embody the love of God. Notice that we are talking about living the law, not merely thinking about it. Deut. 32:46 says, "Take to heart all the words I have solemnly declared to you this day, so that you may command your children to obey carefully all the words of this law."

Third, the law is called a teacher. Paul says in Gal. 3:24-25, "So the law was put in charge to lead us to Christ that we might be justified by faith. Now that faith has come, we are no longer under the supervision of the law." This passage is very important to understanding the relationship between the gospel and the law. Jesus said, "Do not think that I have come to abolish the Law or the Prophets; I have not come to abolish them but to fulfill them" (Matt. 5:17). The New Testament makes it clear that the law, as an expression of God's intent for humanity, is timeless. Jesus came to reclaim the meaning of the law. "The Sabbath was made for man, not man for the Sabbath. So the Son of Man is Lord even of the Sabbath" (Mark 2:27-28).

Fourth, the law helps to define sin. Rom. 7:7 declares, "I would not have known what sin was except through the law."

Paul also says, "But sin is not taken into account when there is no law" (5:13). Even more clearly stated, "Through the law we become conscious of sin" (3:20). Specifically, this means that law serves as our teacher and shows us that what we have been doing is sin. Because of the law each of us becomes aware of our need for God's grace.

Fifth, the law is holy. Paul says in Rom. 7:12, "The law is holy, and the commandment is holy, righteous and good." Isaiah refers to the law as "great and glorious" (42:21). The Psalmist declares, "Oh, how I love your law!" (119:97). This is because, he says, it helps him to avoid the wrong path (v. 104). Ps. 19:7-8 says, "The law of the Lord is perfect, reviving the soul. The statutes of the Lord are trustworthy, making wise the simple. The precepts of the Lord are right, giving joy to the heart. The commands of the Lord are radiant, giving light to the eyes." When we combine the holiness of the law with an understanding of its role in defining sin, we can better understand both aspects.

Sixth, the law is inward. Jer. 31:33 says, "I will put My law within them, and on their heart I will write it" (NASB). The law of Moses was a miraculous event in the history of humankind. It was God revealing himself to a people who had been elected to show the world the righteousness of God. Still the law was located in a tabernacle or a temple. The promise set forth by Jeremiah is that the law will one day be written on the heart of humankind. True obedience to the law comes from within us: "The prophet cannot hope for any change as a result of his own teaching, but only through the creative intervention of Yahweh himself. For he alone can transform the heart of the infatuated, so that they open themselves to his love."[11] We cannot properly understand the law apart from the inward transforming power of God.

These considerations of the law enable us to see the broad picture. The law is the preparation for Christianity, not the ultimate goal to be attained. Too often we have assumed that to keep the law is holiness. But living out the Christian faith is much more than keeping a set of rules, no matter how long the list. Robert Wall sounds an important warning: "We have become a country and a church of legalists in need of liberation from our laws, which often oppress and fail to redeem."[12] Yet this must be balanced against the insightful remark of William Willimon: "But let's be honest: Some of our problems stem from the human penchant to exonerate ourselves from the tough task of behaving like Christians."[13] These two comments should remind us that it is not easy to find the balance between law and grace.

The law is powerless, but grace is limitless. After describing his life under the law, Paul breaks out in thanksgiving, "Therefore, there is now no condemnation for those who are in Christ Jesus, because through Christ Jesus the law of the Spirit of life set me free" (Rom. 8:1-2). The law can describe the Christian life, but it cannot help us live it. The law can define sin, but it cannot offer the power to overcome it. The message of the gospel is that we have been set free by Christ Jesus. The law is not an end unto itself, it is at best a teacher and at worst a milestone. It is only by the grace of God that we have a new law written on our hearts.

Properly understood, the law is not opposed to grace; grace is not opposed to law. They depend on one another, and holding them in tension will allow the Christian to appreciate both more fully. As we suggested at the start of this analysis, neither a "graceless law" nor a "lawless grace" will suffice. Responsible freedom is the alternative to these two perversions of the gospel.

## Called to Be Free

Personal and social liberation is a theme throughout the Scripture. The Exodus account is a vivid reminder of how significant the idea of deliverance is in the Christian tradition. Jesus is described as the Passover in the New Testament (1 Cor. 5:7). Paul lifts the Cross as the symbol of the Christian message. Through all of this is the biblical call to spiritual freedom. In the previous section, we described the parameters of the Christian life: law and grace. Whatever freedom we enjoy is lived between these two poles. Both are essential to what responsible freedom is all about.

An incident from my childhood illustrates responsible freedom. Shortly after I turned 12, my father left me in charge of the household while he and my mother ran an errand. They were planning to be gone for only a few hours, but this was my first time for being the boss. This meant I would be in charge of my two sisters. This newfound freedom was wonderful for a while. But not long after my parents left, we accidentally locked ourselves out of the house. I had to tear the screen in order to get back inside. When my parents got home, I decided to dip into my savings and pay for a new screen, which I helped my father put in the door. I learned a hard lesson about freedom that day—it demands responsibility.

**The Pauline Imperative.** The gospel calls us out of sin into grace, out of darkness into light. Anyone who thinks that the Scripture is soft on sin and tolerant toward wickedness is wrong. Those who have been touched by the redeeming blood of Christ are to be characterized by responsible behavior. Rom. 6:4 says, "We were therefore buried with him through baptism into death in order that, just as Christ was raised from the dead . . . we too may live a new life." Col. 2:6 is equally clear: "Just as you received Christ Jesus as Lord, continue to live in him." The New Testament presents a clear imperative to live the Christian life. There is no ambiguity about where the Scripture stands on the issue of immorality. Jesus said to the woman caught in adultery, "Go now and leave your life of sin" (John 8:11). Peter says, "Be holy in all you do" (1 Pet. 1:15). The Scripture presents a clear call to a holy life.

We must not forget that the call to responsible behavior is rooted in an understanding of grace. The Christian is a child of wrath who by the grace of God has become a new being. The glorious truth is that this new being is called into a new way of living. This path is characterized by faithful obedience to God. Such a life is properly described as a fulfillment of the law. Rom. 14:17 presents this very clearly: "For the kingdom of God is not a matter of eating and drinking, but of righteousness, peace and joy in the Holy Spirit."

81

What does the Pauline imperative imply for sexual ethics? First, it means that what one does sexually is linked to religious values. Sexuality is not a special case, excluded from the parameters of morality. On the other hand, sexuality is not to be lifted up as the only area of interest to moral reflection. While sexuality is important, it is not the only place where the Scriptures speak. I'm not convinced, however, that we should avoid asking hard questions concerning sexuality because other issues remain unresolved. For example, some would argue that questions concerning homosexuality should not be addressed because we do not talk about gluttony with equal enthusiasm. Perhaps both issues should be addressed instead of neither.

Second, it means that sexuality should be a vehicle that shows to the world who God is. In the Christian context, sexuality is a gift to be cherished, not merely a passion to be controlled. Therefore, we should work toward bringing our Christianity and our sexuality together. This includes control but goes far beyond it. In fact, *"All* sexual behavior or conduct requires a measure of *control* if it is to be realized at its best."[14] It is no mistake that Paul spends so much time on the issue of sexuality. The problem and possibility of sexuality lies very close to the center of who we are as human beings. Because of this it will require special diligence to act "Christianly" toward members of the opposite sex.

Third, it requires a "morality of caution." This raises two questions: "Am I likely to get hurt? . . . Am I likely to hurt someone else?"[15] An ethic that grows out of the Pauline imperative must learn to ask about consequences. This will mean, in part, that we will have to learn how to be unselfish with our actions. We must be "other-directed," instead of "me-centered."

On a practical level this means that the way we treat people should reflect our sense of moral responsibility. In *The Republic,* which is one of the more influential books in Western philosophy, a person argues that people are "just" because they value a good reputation. In order to support his contention, the person arguing with Socrates tells a story where the "just" person has a ring that can make him invisible. He asserts that the "just" person, when given the opportunity to behave unjustly and suffer no consequences, will do so. In other words, when a person is given the freedom to behave immorally and get away with it, he will. The modern world has given to many what appears to be the ability to have sexual relations and suffer no consequences. We need to be reminded that a Christian is called to a different kind of life, one in which we are free in the context of responsibility to one another and to God.

These three implications help us understand the nature of Christian responsibility. They focus our attention upon the meaning of obedience to the law. It is only in the context of caution, concern, grace, relationship, and law that we fully realize what God intended for us to be. Responsibility is the element that enables us to experience freedom.

**Freedom.** One of the most interesting books in the Bible is Galatians. Here Paul is presenting the gospel again to some new Christians who are wishing to return to Judaism. It is inconceivable to Paul that those who had known the grace of God would want to return to the law. He writes, "It is for freedom that Christ has set us free. Stand firm, then, and do not let yourselves be burdened again by a yoke of slavery" (5:1). Prior to saying this, Paul has already presented the fact that "Christ redeemed us from the curse of the law by becoming a curse for us" (3:13). He says further, "Before this faith came, we were held prisoners by the law, locked up until faith should be revealed" (v. 23). Clearly, the good news of the gospel is that we are free from legalism.

But what does freedom really mean? First, it means that we have recovered an appreciation of the absolute. Paul is not suggesting that the gospel implies abolishing the law. Jesus came to fulfill the law, not to destroy it. It is lazy thinking that would make the gospel a "Do as you please" ethic. Christians are not left without resources to live the holy life. We must never allow the circumstances of our world to determine our life-style. American society is a great example of a people madly reaching after the newest fancy. For many, life is captured in the phrase from a bumper sticker: "The one who dies with the most toys wins the game." There is no freedom in abolishing our sense of absolute value.

Second, we need to be reminded that the law is tempered by grace. When we think of the law, there is a tendency to think in terms of "Thou shalt" and "Thou shalt not." But the very existence of the law is a testimony to the fact that God loves His people. While the direct commandments are not always the easiest to follow or accept, they increase freedom. The person who chooses to drink and drive is certainly free to do so. But the consequences may result in less freedom, not more. A friend recently observed that many of his classmates in law school had several sexual partners each year. He insightfully added, "They are really taking quite a chance!" Often what lies at the end of that road is not freedom but bondage.

The secular mind-set preaches the gospel of indulgence: "Get all you can while you can!" This gives the message that all our problems can be solved with "something." The credo here is "I am free to do whatever I please, with whomever I please, no matter what it costs!" The world exists for my pleasure. Indeed, there is a sense in which we are free to indulge ourselves. We can play the game until we forget why we are playing.

The freedom available in Christ arises from several insights. First, God's power is always sufficient for the task. This means that the gift of sexuality, which comes from God, need not frustrate our spiritual quest. In fact, there is grace from God to make the gift of sexuality a reflection of His creativity.

Second, God calls us to do something with our lives. It is not enough to reinforce all the don'ts concerning sexual behavior. God calls us to do more with our sexuality than say, "No!" Because we are free in God's grace, we are called to use our sexuality to mirror the joyous relation of God to His creation. Sexuality should be a positive reflection of our origin in God. It is time for the Christian to stand up and say, "It is possible to be sexual and Christian at the same time." A number of years ago there was a popular song that asked, "Why should the devil have all the good music?" If that question applies to music, it certainly applies to sexuality, which is a good gift from God signifying our relationship with the Creator. It is more than a device of the devil to frustrate adolescents. It is the call to be fully human, fully alive, and fully Christian. When one answers this call within the context of marriage, all that God intended our sexual existence to be can be realized.

Romans 14 presents an interesting postscript to our discussion. Paul suggests that Christian freedom is really not an individual undertaking. For the Christian, freedom means more than claiming one's rights; it is seeking to do that which "leads to peace and to mutual edification" (v. 19). In other words, Christian freedom is tied to the community of faith. Paul can say, therefore, "All food is clean, but it is wrong for a man to eat anything that causes someone else to stumble" (v. 20). Where sexuality is concerned, the message is clear. My sexual freedom really is not liberation until it includes the other. While we cannot be constrained by another person's misunderstandings, we shouldn't ignore our brother or sister. A paradox of the Christian faith is that when we bear others' burdens, we find true freedom. Could it be that this paradigm opens up the true meaning of sexual expression? Could it be that such responsibility is freedom?

## Summary

1. The Christian life is lived between the parameters of law and grace. This avoids the extremes of a "graceless law" and a "lawless grace." This is the fundamental tension of the Christian life. The expression "Law is grace" captures the fundamental tension between law and grace.

2. An understanding of grace is essential to a full appreciation of the gospel.

3. Grace is the acceptance of God's love and implies the responsibility to share it.

4. Law helps to give love a structure in the Christian life.

5. Ultimately, law and grace complement one another in the Christian life.

6. For the Christian, freedom is fully understood in the context of responsibility.

# Notes

1. Geoffrey W. Bromiley, *Theological Dictionary of the New Testament*, 1-vol. ed. (Grand Rapids: William B. Eerdmans Publishing Co., 1985), 1304.

2. Ibid., 1301.

3. Ibid., 1301-2.

4. William Greathouse and H. Ray Dunning, *An Introduction to Wesleyan Theology*, rev. and enl. ed. (Kansas City: Beacon Hill Press of Kansas City, 1989), 73.

5. Robert Trainer, "Love," in *Baker's Dictionary of Christian Ethics*, ed. Carl F. H. Henry (Grand Rapids: Canon Press, 1973), 396.

6. James Gustafson, *Theology and Christian Ethics* (Philadelphia: A Pilgrim Press Book, 1974), 71.

7. Mildred Bangs Wynkoop, *A Theology of Love: The Dynamic of Wesleyanism* (Kansas City: Beacon Hill Press of Kansas City, 1972), 33.

8. O. Raymond Jonston, "Law," in *Baker's Dictionary of Theology*, ed. Everett F. Harrison (Grand Rapids: Baker Book House, 1960), 317.

9. C. M. Horne, "Law in the New Testament," in *The Zondervan Pictorial Encyclopedia of the Bible*, ed. Merrill C. Tenney, 5 vols. (Grand Rapids: Zondervan Publishing House, 1975), 3:894.

10. W. A. Whitehouse, *Justice and Law* (London: SCM Press, 1955), 14.

11. Walther Eichrodt, *A Theology of the Old Testament*, trans. J. A. Baker, 2 vols. (Philadelphia: Westminster Press, 1961), 2:295.

12. Robert Wall, "The Liberated Legalist," *Christian Century* (Sept. 28, 1983): 849.

13. William Willimon, "The Limits of Kindness," *Christian Century* (Apr. 14, 1982): 447.

14. W. Norman Pittenger, *Love and Control in Sexuality* (Philadelphia: United Church Press, 1974), 31.

15. Smedes, *Sex for Christians*, 118.

# 5

# The Question of Homosexuality

The sexual revolution raised many significant issues. Teenage sexuality, marriage and divorce, the role of the church in sex education, and the role of culture in shaping Christian faith and morality are just a few. One issue underlies all the others: What does Christian morality have to do with the emerging insights of the sciences, including psychology? One sexual taboo after another has disappeared during the last 30 years. Largely this happened because of the cultural dispositions described in the first chapter: secular humanism, alienation, technology, and relativism. A sense of uneasiness has led many theologians to wait for science to speak before they take a position.

The conflict between science, ethics, and theology becomes most evident in the question of homosexuality. No doubt, "Homosexuality . . . challenges us in different ways, according to our own personalities and relationships. The challenge hits us at the deepest, most hidden level of ourselves: how do we handle our own sexuality?"[1] Recent medical research has called into question the Church's traditional stand on homosexuality. We must examine this issue because it symbolizes the most fundamental problem confronting evangelical theology/ethics.

There is genuine confusion concerning homosexuality on the part of many evangelicals. Harold Greenlee says that nowhere does Jesus "give the slightest basis for assuming that he considered homosexual unions . . . to be an acceptable lifestyle."[2] On the other hand Virginia Mollenkott says, "Homosexual Christians can enter a same-sex union without breaking the cohumanity of creation."[3] The usual evangelical response is to deny any compatibility between Christian morality and the practice of homosexuality. Most denominations take an adamant stance, yet within the ranks of pastors, counselors, physicians, and others who seek to faithfully minister in the church, there is confusion.

The Scripture clearly condemns homosexual behavior. Lev. 20:13 expresses the biblical point of view: "If a man lies with a man as one lies with a woman, both of them have done what is detestable. They must be put to death." Rom. 1:26-27 provides an equally clear statement: "Because of this, God gave them over to shameful lusts. Even their women exchanged natural relations for unnatural ones. In the same way the men also abandoned natural relations with women and were inflamed with lust for one another. Men committed indecent acts with other men, and received in themselves the due penalty for their perversion." According to Victor Furnish, homosexuality is not "a fundamental biblical theme . . . We have to hunt for relevant passages."[4] Yet he has no trouble concluding that Paul saw "homosexual conduct . . . [as] . . . symptomatic of an individual's fundamental refusal to acknowledge God."[5]

The New Testament uses two words for homosexuality: *arsenokoita* and *malakoi.*[6] The first term is used in Rom. 1:27 and always connotes a homosexual act. Literally, it means sodomite, and it implies the practice of anal intercourse between males. Paul has in mind the Roman practice of pederasty. Here a younger boy will voluntarily enter into a sexual relationship with an older male for the purpose of gratifying the older partner. This kind of relationship often existed between a Roman soldier and a young boy who would accompany him on military campaigns. This was widely practiced in the Greco/Roman world. The second term is used in 1 Cor. 6:9 and refers to voluptuous persons. Literally, the term means soft or effeminate. This term is used in Matt. 11:8 to refer to men who wear silk and satin. Perhaps the best translation of this word *(malakoi)* is pervert. Both types of homosexuality were practiced in the Roman Empire; both are condemned in the New Testament.

The genuine confusion concerning homosexuality arises less from theology than from personal associations. No one feels sympathy for the male who dresses like a female and marches in a gay-pride parade. We may sympathize with a woman who was sexually abused by her father and then by her husband. We can understand her confusion when the first real warmth she has experienced comes from another woman. As long as homosexuality remains a principle, it can be easily handled. But when the principle has a name, things become more difficult. These unfortunate circumstances do not justify homosexuality but help explain the present confusion.

The Church has traditionally assumed that most, if not all, homosexuality is voluntary. A growing body of scientific data suggests that, at least for some, homosexuality is not a choice. For those who are attempting to act as Christian counselors, there is often a conflict between "good theology" and "good psychology" or "good medicine." The homosexual question places Christians in many human service professions in conflict with their academic training.

A clear understanding of homosexuality is essential to any moral analysis of homosexual behavior. Homosexuality is "a predominant, persistent, and exclusive psychosexual attraction toward members of the same sex."[7] Homosexuality really represents a range of people from the exclusive homosexual to the bisexual, and some suggest this represents about 10 percent of the population.[8] It is an emotionally charged movement that presents a significant challenge to the Christian church. At the base of the discussion is the debate over whether homosexuality is inescapable for some people. Are people, in fact, born with a homosexual tendency that makes all heterosexual desires unlikely? Could it be that due to sexual abuse as a child, an adult is inescapably homosexual? Is homosexuality a biologically or psychologically grounded tendency? Is homosexual behavior a sinful choice that expresses a desire to have it all? These questions must be faced before any relevant moral analysis can take place. According to D. L. Creson, a clinical psychologist: "A satisfactory explanation of homosexuality is not now possible. The bewildering array of psychological, physiological, and sociological variables that appear relevant to any such explanation have yet to be drawn together into an internally consistent model that explains homosexuality."[9] With this in mind, let's look at several possible explanations for homosexuality.

## Explanations

**Hormonal.** This view holds that homosexuality arises due to the presence of certain hormones in the brain. An early pioneer in the scientific study of homosexuality was Havelock Ellis, *Sexual Inversion* (1898, 1936). He hypothesized a physiological explanation for homosexual behavior. Some scientists attribute this to "prenatal hormonal influences on the brain."[10] One scientific survey makes the following assertions:

1. If there is a biological basis for homosexuality, it probably operates more powerfully for exclusive homosexuals than for bisexuals.
2. If there is a biological basis for homosexuality, it probably accounts for gender nonconformity as well as for sexual orientation.
3. If there is a biological basis for homosexuality, it makes it difficult to argue for familial factors.[11]

If these theories are true, homosexuality is a biological condition that predisposes some people to a specific desire that resists change.[12]

**Psychosocial.** This explanation is marked by a great deal of diversity. Male homosexuality is explained on the basis of a detached, hostile father and a seductive mother. The rise of male homosexuality is linked to the degraded status of women, as happened in Greece. Another explanation for homosexuality is the presence of male deities in society. Male homosexuality is said by some to be more likely when available women are too few or too chaste. Male homosexuality is related to difficulty with accumulating enough wealth to acquire a wife. Lesbianism is linked by some to deprived access to heterosexual affection or intimacy, due to shyness, feelings of inadequacy, fears of rejection, or lack of available men.[13] Some see a relationship between homosexuality and highly urbanized societies.[14] Many of these explanations seem implausible but illustrate the diversity of opinion.

One extensive study attempted to understand sexual preference among both males and females. This study linked male homosexuality to negative feelings toward the father. Lesbianism was linked to cold, weak, and detached fathers. The conclusion of these researchers is that "sexual preference is likely to be established quite early in life and that childhood and adolescent sexual expressions by and large reflect rather than determine a person's sexual preference."[15]

Gender nonconformity is often linked to homosexual behavior. This is a disruption of the normal developmental process that leads to specifically masculine and feminine traits. We expect a boy to play with a truck, a toy gun, a basketball, and so on. When the boy picks up a doll, this is considered to be gender nonconformity. Some would hypothesize that a boy who was raised by his mother and played only with girls during the formative years would have trouble conforming to traditional gender-related activities. This might in turn push him toward an uneasiness with his male peers and eventually toward homosexual behavior. This process could work with girls in much the same way.

The psychosocial explanation of homosexuality can lead to the following conclusions. First, homosexuality is rooted in a poor family experience. A poor relationship with the father or mother can manifest itself in homosexuality. Second, gender nonconformity relates to homosexual behavior in many cases. Third, in some cases a traumatic sexual experience (molestation) very early in life can lead to homosexual behavior. It is possible such an early trauma could lead to a total change in sexual orientation.

**Theological.** This position attempts to relate homosexuality to the Fall. The argument goes something like this: God created humankind in His image. During this period humans (Adam and Eve) had perfect fellowship with God. If this relationship had continued without interruption, all people would have lived in obedience to God and in harmony with His creation. Sadly, this fellowship was broken by the free choice of humankind (Adam).

The break in the relationship between God and His creation is essentially the attempt on the part of Adam to transcend the limits. This act of disobedience, instead of making humankind more like God, actually severed the perfect fellowship. The result was a loss of relationship and the nurturing growth that would have followed. Every person, all cultures, and human existence have been affected by this loss of fellowship. Because of this estrangement the human condition has suffered murder, war, hatred, envy, and so on. Our sexual existence has suffered as a part of this history. Therefore sex, which should be a joyous experience provided by the Creator, often is vain worship of the creature. Child abuse, premarital sex, adultery, and other perversions reflect this tragic shift.

Homosexuality, then, is one manifestation of a sickness that indicates an enmity between creature and Creator. The solution to the problem is to be found in the healing grace provided in the resurrection of Jesus. One may be forgiven for all immoral sexual acts by God through faith. Yet the deeper problem may take a lifetime to correct. God's grace and the healing presence of the Christian community are the only hope of dealing with the problem. Where homosexuality is concerned, the healing may only be evident in the ability to refrain from "same sex" intimacy. This commitment to a moral life-style may be painful, but it is possible in the life of grace.

## Moral or Immoral?

**The Argument for Homosexual Behavior** asserts, simply, that homosexual behavior is normal. John Boswell suggests that Christianity did not originally develop a hostile relationship to homosexuals.[16] They blame biblical literalism for the rejection of homosexuality. Scroggs contends that "biblical judgments against homosexuality are not relevant to today's debate."[17] He goes on to add that this does not diminish the authority of Scripture, rather it recognizes that "it does not address the issues involved."[18]

Those who wish to argue for the morality of homosexuality from the Christian point of view must deal with biblical material. Specifically, they must deal with the passages in Leviticus, Romans, 1 Corinthians, and 1 Timothy. Here they assert that Leviticus condemns sodomy, whether it is homosexual or heterosexual. They understand that Romans, 1 Corinthians, and 1 Timothy are actually condemning any adult/child relationship that is homosexual (pederasty). They conclude that the Scripture does not condemn monogamous homosexual behavior. Beyond this they suggest that the Bible would bless any loving, life-affirming relationship that is characterized by fidelity and mutual respect. They assert that many homosexual relationships are characterized in this manner.

Another argument supporting homosexual behavior relies on personhood. Some psychologists feel that once a homosexual is known not by a label but personally, he will more likely be accepted. Rinzema suggests "that Christian moralists develop a morality for homosexuality in consultation with homosexual people."[19] One psychologist pointed out to me that some homosexuals get physically sick when they attempt to be close to a person of the opposite sex. She went on to suggest that it would be immoral to require such a person to be anything other than a homosexual. When homosexuals are seen as normal people, all prohibitions against homosexual behavior will be abolished.

Homosexuality is supported on the basis of the oppression apparent in sexual roles. Some feminists believe that heterosexuality is a mechanism for the oppression of women. They say this oppression is evidenced in laws that favor monogamous, heterosexual marital relationships.[20] According to this argument, homosexual behavior is the only reliable way to step out of sexual roles and thus oppression.

**The Argument Against Homosexuality** asserts that the Christian tradition has never affirmed homosexual behavior. It suggests that positions such as those offered by Boswell confuse tolerance with acceptance. Lev. 18:22 says, "Do not lie with a man as one lies with a woman; that is detestable." Lev. 20:13 requires death for homosexual behavior. Paul specifically mentions homosexual offenders in 1 Cor. 6:9-10. This biblical prohibition is carried into the Early Church. It seems abundantly clear that all homosexual behavior is condemned in the Scripture and in the tradition that follows. While some argue that Paul is condemning homosexual prostitutes, not all homosexual relationships, most scholars agree that the Church has never condoned homosexual behavior.

Those who oppose homosexual behavior say that it is unnatural—that God intends sexual intimacy to take place between male and female. Taking this into account, Thielicke suggests that "Christian pastoral care will have to be concerned primarily with helping the person to sublimate homosexual urge."[21] Marc Oraison feels that "homosexual desire itself is rooted in the aggravation of an already painful narcissism."[22] Since homosexual love denies that God-intended pattern, it can never seek the other's good. Accordingly, it can be an act of compassion for the Christian to hold out for the healing love of God's grace for the homosexual. Helping a person to resist homosexual behavior does not have to be done in a judgmental way. The fundamental assertion is that all homosexual behavior is unnatural when viewed from the Christian perspective.

A final argument is that homosexual behavior encourages irresponsibility in a way that heterosexual relationships do not. The pattern in the male homosexual community has tended to be characterized by numerous partners. Sexual activity is purely for pleasure and never for procreation. It cannot be intimate on the spiritual level. The plain fact that God created the two sexes for intimate fellowship argues against homosexuality. When "same sex" acts are substituted for heterosexual relations, they are not responsible to God's creation.

## Conclusions

As the title of this chapter suggests, homosexuality presents us with a question. Homosexuals are coming out of the closet in our time. The winds of change produced by the sexual revolution have influenced attitudes toward homosexuality. Books, television, and the movies make us aware that there are vast numbers of homosexuals, many of whom are in positions of influence. Two members of the United States Congress have admitted to being homosexual; one has since been reelected. What is a Christian to make of this changing attitude toward homosexuality?

The first question raised by the issue is biblical authority. What are we to think about those passages that specifically condemn homosexual behavior? Proponents of homosexual behavior say that the biblical prohibitions are so specific they only refer to sodomy and pederasty (child molesting). They also argue that slavery, racism, and sexism have all been supported by using the Bible.

Those who oppose homosexual behavior interpret the biblical passages concerning homosexuality as relating to all homosexual contact. The real question is related to biblical authority. Is the Bible, which was written in a different cultural situation, relevant today? Does it make a difference if biblical writers did not know about monogamous homosexual relationships? Could it be that the Bible contains a wisdom beyond our understanding?

Second, how important is experience to theological/ethical understanding? Some say it is a lack of contact with homosexuals that allows us to condemn the activity. They contend that when divorce came to the evangelical church, the hard condemnation vanished. They say that contact with people of other ethnic origins has forced the church to reconsider racial prejudice.

Those who oppose homosexual behavior point out that many former homosexuals say it is possible to change with God's grace. They suggest that sympathy for those we love might push us to affirm immorality on occasion. Who would want to condemn a lifelong friend who admits to homosexual feelings and behavior? Perhaps the Christian attitude should be one of accepting the homosexual into the healing ministry of the church. Could it be that more contact with homosexuals would lead, not to accepting their life-style, but to healing?

At this point it is important to note that the principle of self-respect or creation is the most powerful argument against homosexuality. Put very simply, God created man and woman for sexual fellowship. The fact that some heterosexual relationships are exploitative does not legitimize homosexuality. The Fall has affected all relationships, but homosexual contact is not affirmed in creation. The nearly 2,000 years of Christian reflection agrees that God's pattern of sexual intimacy is heterosexual.

After looking at the evidence, the only valid conclusion is that any homosexual behavior is immoral. This means the homosexual who has numerous sexual contacts. It also includes long-term homosexual relationships. Even though such relationships are committed, they deny the original plan of God for human fellowship.

The questions regarding homosexuality are multi-layered. The purpose of these pages has been to examine the theological and ethical resources for coming to grips with homosexual behavior. We should never lose sight of the anguish represented by the person who feels trapped by homosexual desires. Several years ago I attended a conference sponsored by an evangelical college. One of the special interest groups addressed homosexuality. The speaker characterized the problem and attempted to account for homosexuality. At this point a young man spoke up, "By that analysis I should be heterosexual, but I'm not." The gasps in the room were audible. By his attitude it was evident that this man was not a practicing homosexual but daily had to deal with homosexual desires and homosexual behavior.

Another often-overlooked person is the evangelical parent of a homosexual. What must it be like to be told by a child that he is homosexual? Certainly guilt and anger surge to the surface. We in the evangelical church can be of assistance as we help parents of homosexuals to know the healing grace of God. It is not our purpose to, with folded arms, condemn others. We simply cannot allow those parents to suffer alone. A climate of trust and redemption should characterize the church. When this happens, people can share their burdens with the community of faith.

The Christian position on homosexuality is one of God's healing grace. The church should not reject homosexuals. A great many people through no conscious choice have homosexual desires. The church in its desire and responsibility to reject the homosexual life-style should not alienate the homosexual. Rather, it should reach out in love with the message of healing grace. The church, and thus the Christian, has no part in the hatred and fear that cause people to attack, physically or emotionally, the homosexual. Yet the message must be lived and preached that the Creator is not honored in homosexual behavior.

## Summary

1. Homosexuality is a diverse and difficult problem that must be addressed by the church in a creative manner.

2. The question raised by homosexuality is causing a good deal of confusion in the church.

3. Homosexuality can be explained in at least three ways: hormonal, psychosocial, and theological. These explanations are not necessarily mutually exclusive.

4. A careful consideration of all the information must lead to the conclusion that all homosexual behavior is inconsistent with Christian morality.

5. The church must reach out in love to the homosexual in the hope of God's healing grace.

## Notes

1. Marc Oraison, *The Homosexual Question*, trans. Jane Zeni Flinn (New York: Harper and Row, Publishers, 1977), 1.

2. J. Harold Greenlee, "The New Testament and Homosexuality," in *What You Should Know About Homosexuality*, ed. Charles W. Keyson (Grand Rapids: Zondervan Publishing House, 1979), 83.

3. Letha Scanzoni and Virginia Mollenkott, *Is the Homosexual My Neighbor?: Another Christian View* (New York: Harper and Row, Publishers, 1978), 130.

4. Victor Paul Furnish, *The Moral Teaching of Paul: Selected Issues* (Nashville: Abingdon Press, 1979, 1985), 53.

5. Ibid., 78.

6. Derrick Sherwin Bailey, *Homosexuality and the Western Christian Tradition* (London: Archon Books, 1975), 156; also Robin Scroggs, *The New Testament and Homosexuality* (Philadelphia: Fortress Press, 1983), 106-9.

7. George A. Kanoti and Anthony R. Kosnik, "Homosexuality—Ethical Aspects," in *Encyclopedia of Bioethics,* vol. 2, ed. Warren T. Reich (New York: Free Press, 1978), 671.

8. Lee Birk, "The Myth of Classical Homosexuality: Views of a Behavioral Psychotherapist," in *Homosexual Behavior: A Modern Reappraisal,* ed. Judd Marmor (New York: Basic Books, Publishers, 1980), 376.

9. D. L. Creson, "Homosexuality—Clinical and Behavioral Aspects," in *Encyclopedia of Bioethics,* 669.

10. John Money, "Genetic and Chromosomal Aspects of Homosexual Etiology," in *Homosexual Behavior,* 69-70.

11. Alan P. Bell, Martin S. Weinberg, and Sue Kiefer Hammersmith, *Sexual Preference: Its Development in Men and Women* (Bloomington, Ind.: Indiana University Press, 1981), 216-18.

12. Ibid., 222.

13. Judd Marmor, "Overview: The Multiple Roots of Homosexual Behavior," in *Homosexual Behavior,* 10-18.

14. John Boswell, *Christianity, Social Tolerance, and Homosexuality: Gay People in Western Europe from the Beginning of the Christian Era to the Fourteenth Century* (Chicago and London: University of Chicago Press, 1980), 35.

15. Bell, Weinberg, and Hammersmith, *Sexual Preference,* 113.

16. Boswell, *Homosexuality,* 135.

17. Scroggs, *Homosexuality,* 127.

18. Ibid.

19. J. Rinzema, *The Sexual Revolution: Challenge and Response,* trans. Lewis Smedes (Grand Rapids: William B. Eerdmans Publishing Co., 1974), 106.

20. E. Carrington Boggan et al., *The Rights of Gay People: The Basic ACLU Guide to a Gay Person's Rights* (Toronto and Vancouver, B.C.: A Richard Baron Book, 1975), 103.

21. Helmut Thielicke, *The Ethics of Sex,* trans. John W. Doberstein (New York: Harper and Row, Publishers, 1964), 287.

22. Oraison, *Homosexual Question,* 53.

# 6

# The Revolution
# and Its Lessons

The sexual revolution presents two very powerful images. One is of a person who is emotionally scarred or physically diseased. Sexual exploitation has led to a life of pain and isolation for this person. This is a very powerful reminder that sexual license is bondage, not freedom. The second image is of a healthy person who is in touch with his sexuality. This person has grown through the sexual revolution to become more of what God intended. For this person sexual intercourse has become a way of seeing God's grace. It is only in God that love, relationship, and commitment come into focus. Therefore, God's grace is most clearly understood on a human level in terms of a loving relationship. These two images must be kept in tension to understand the significance of the sexual revolution.

In chapter 1 I suggested that while we hear less about the sexual revolution these days, the real revolution has only begun. The following chapters established principles for dealing with the sexual revolution: self-respect, love, and responsible freedom. It is not enough for Christians to stand in the pulpit and decry the sad situation of our world. We need to emphasize that there are a number of lessons to be learned from the sexual revolution.

1. **A positive view of sexuality.** Perhaps the most important lesson we can learn is to celebrate our sexuality. It will be tragic if the secular mind-set is successful in its attempt to say that Christianity is antisexuality. The God-given ability for sexual expression must not be surrendered to those who would abuse it. The Christian ought to learn how to emphasize the positive dimension of sexuality. It is not a burden, it is rather a pathway to a fuller appreciation of God's relationship to creation. It is correct to assert "that there is *no reason in principle* why Christian faith must be polarized into spiritual and material, into eternal and temporal."[1] We do not have to make a choice between spirituality and sexuality. The whole point of the gospel is to tear down such division. It is even possible to see that "God intends increasing sexual wholeness to be part of our redemption."[2] A growing relationship with God should include an appreciation of one's sexuality.

Several years ago it was my good pleasure to encounter an elderly minister. He had just returned from a ministers' conference where a friend of mine had been the principal speaker. Naturally I was interested to hear about the conference. The minister said quickly, "There wasn't much to it! He talked about theology. What we really needed was psychology." This was a little shocking to me but probably represents the opinion of many. For some people theology has lost its appeal, and perhaps the theologian is to blame for some of this attitude. Theology can become a boring enterprise, filled with irrelevant speculation. At the same time, we should be careful not to underestimate the power of the gospel. This is exactly what theology is—the attempt to more fully appreciate the gospel. This includes the integration of body and mind, of sexuality and theology. When theology is in touch with life, people will listen.

An affirmation of sexuality will lead us away from isolation toward interpersonal love. All people fear rejection. To be alone is not pleasant; yet today many people are isolated, even in our large cities. Sexuality is at one level a gentle reminder that God intends fellowship. This can be a path toward liberation. Within the context of marriage it is possible to experience the true meaning of love, the joy of communion, and the essence of liberation. This is only possible through the enduring truth that sexuality is God's gift. The church must not forget "how to affirm the mystery and goodness of sex."[3] When we do find ways of affirming sexuality, the whole communal existence of our faith will be enhanced.

The answer to the sexual revolution is not a more subtle set of arguments against perversion. At least part of the answer is to be found in maintaining a positive image of sexuality in the church. We need to seek ways to express the goodness and mystery of sexuality. The best sex education occurs in the home with Christian parents. Perhaps the church could find ways of equipping young parents for dealing with solid principles concerning sexuality. A similar method of instruction is necessary for Sunday School teachers, and not just junior and senior high level. We should build a positive image of sexuality while our children are young, because even 11- and 12-year-olds are being forced to make tough choices concerning sex. We must equip ourselves to confront the difficult choices that people must make in relation to sexuality.

Several years ago after preaching a sermon at camp meeting on affirming our sexuality, an 85-year-old woman approached me. It was with some measure of anxiety that I shook her hand. One could easily assume that she had been offended by my remarks. Instead, she looked me squarely in the eyes and said, "I wish somebody had told me that 60 years ago!" This incident has led me to conclude that each of us must summon the courage to speak the truth in love. It would be a tragedy if even a single person under the church's influence misunderstands his sexuality. Perhaps he is waiting for somebody to tell him.

2. **Recover a healthy sense of the absolute.** We have already discussed the problems associated with relativism and pluralism. For many, the credo is "The truth is whatever I say it is!" Mass communication, secularism, and the like have convinced some that no ultimate values exist. We treated the theological perspective represented by Mark C. Taylor known as postmodernism. All of this suggests that the church

needs to be aware of its responsibility to stand for some absolutes. Yet the true mission of the church is to deal with lonely and confused people. To these people the Sunday School teacher may say, "Don't have sex until you are married." But the world is saying, "It feels good, so go ahead!" Many people, both teenagers and beyond, are confused about how to order their life. Some would even advise that the proper procedure is to stick your finger in the air to see which way the wind is blowing. The clear message of the Scripture is that we have better resources for moral living.

I came to realize the importance of absolutes during my years of graduate study. A respected member of the religion faculty underscored the importance of solid values in a lecture I once heard. He said, "If I had to do it all over again, I would raise my children in the most conservative church in town." This was an astonishing statement coming from a man who had invested all of his life in radical theology. Later in the lecture, he made it clear he was not advocating the conservative point of view. But he was concerned that his children did not have any solid ground to stand upon. The message that there are no absolute values translates for a child into "I can do anything I want to." A belief in absolutes is the faith that there is light, even when it appears we are groping in the darkness. The minute a person begins to feel that only darkness exists, the entire fabric of the moral life unravels.

One of the obstacles to a healthy view of absolutes is feeling that the law is a burden. Sometimes we tend to see only "Thou shalt" and "Thou shalt not." But behind these rules stands a God who loves His children enough to provide a sense of direction. He gives His law to us because He is gracious. We must resist with every fiber of our being the tendency to be legalistic, but with equal intensity we must resist antinomianism. The gospel lies between the poles of legalism and irresponsibility.

During the spring of 1987 I traveled to England. This was a trip of a lifetime for me. My oldest daughter, Shelly, accompanied me. She was nine at the time but seemed to get some good out of looking at all the John Wesley sites. Shelly had never been away from her mother, so I knew that this

10-day tour would seem a long time to her. About halfway through the trip we were in York, England. The York Minster, a beautiful church, stands very near to the center of this city. It is second only to the Westminster Cathedral in importance to the Church of England. Shelly and I toured this great structure. It is in every way an amazing place.

When we left the church, it seemed good to call Boston and talk with my wife. During our short telephone conversation my wife informed me that our youngest daughter, Megan, had been taken to the emergency room two days earlier. She was at home now, but this little bit of news was painful. When I hung up the phone, Shelly burst into tears. Not only did she miss her mother, but now her 18-month-old sister was sick. It was difficult to console her, because I was about to cry too. We walked rather aimlessly through the streets of York, trying to think. Suddenly Shelly and I were in front of the York Minster. This time, however, it was not a structure to be admired, but a house of prayer. This time we sat in the beautiful church and prayed for Megan.

As I reflect on this incident, it reminds me of an important distinction concerning the law. We can admire the law as an impressive achievement. Legal scholars can debate its precepts. But for the law to be effective, it must be more than an object of admiration, it must be written in our hearts. Just as the York Minster was transformed from a big building into a house of prayer, the law must become personal. The absolute must be more than something we discuss, it must be something we live.

A certain amount of courage is necessary for setting forth absolutes. At every level we must be careful not to allow fanaticism to characterize our ethics. Some things are not absolute, and it is a mistake to try and make them so. But without certain absolutes we are cast into the nothingness of our own imagination. Yet taking a stand for morality requires courage because the broader cultural mood rejects any absolute moral value.

A healthy appreciation of absolutes will include a conviction that a real difference between right and wrong exists. It will free us from the frantic search for meaning. It will also unite the spiritual, the moral, and the theological. An appreciation for absolutes will drive us into the Scripture again. The issue will not be the existence of lasting values, but an attempt to define them. It is time for Christians to be about the task of determining what values are important. Most will fall somewhere between two poles. First, we must avoid fanatical absolutism. This view tries to make every detail of life into an absolute value. Often this mentality characterizes people who struggle with doubt. For them the answer is to deny all questions, even the legitimate ones. Second, we must avoid relativism. This view attempts to deny any and all lasting values. The balance is a person who is open to discover all of God's truth. This includes doubt, but it ultimately leads to greater clarity. A healthy view of absolutes does not require a termination of thought. It frees us to live in a world of doubt with the peace of God.

3. **Hear the Scripture anew.** Every new generation needs to confront the Scripture again. It is never enough to rely upon the interpretations and experience of others. We must read the Bible for ourselves. This will keep us in touch with its radical message. Perhaps this will keep us from "tying the gospel . . . to any intellectual construct."[4] Americanism, capitalism, conservatism, and liberalism often obstruct our understanding of the Bible. The Scripture transcends all of this and speaks to us where we are. When the message of the Scripture is clearly presented, a decision will have to be made: "To communicate the Gospel means putting it before the people so that they are able to decide for or against it. The Christian gospel is a matter of decision."[5] The sexual revolution has forced a new study of the Scripture. As we explore, we will find a "new healing reality."[6] This reality will help us to chart a path in this perilous time. We can certainly agree with Nancy Barcus, "It is time to reclaim, to exercise, the heritage of the Christian mind."[7]

All of this points back to the need for consistent dialogue. Memorizing Scripture passages will not suffice. We must find a way to communicate the Scriptures as we are open to meaningful dialogue with others: "In the revolution confronting us, the real test of any theological or ethical perspective will be its ability to recognize fully the importance of the insights of the experts and to contribute something in the dialogue with him."[8] When the message of Scripture is understood, the Christian can with confidence seek to be in dialogue. There can be little doubt that "Christians today are inescapably confronted with the need to *think* about the standards of sexual behavior which they ought to proclaim and practice."[9]

The dialogue advocated here will require that theology, psychology, and sociology learn from one another. Our society wholeheartedly endorses the values of both psychology and sociology. Talk shows regularly host experts in both of these disciplines. People consult a psychotherapist the way they consulted a pastor years ago. The cultural shift to these disciplines is not all bad, but one dimension is omitted—the spiritual. Only when we bring theology and the Christian faith to the discussion table will a well-rounded discussion ensue. We have already mentioned Phil Donohue's television special "The Human Animal." It was in many ways a very interesting experience to watch. He was attempting to describe humanity as fully as possible. In order to do this, he talked to intellectual historians, anthropologists, psychologists, medical researchers, sociologists, and the like. He discussed topics that ranged from sex to war and from nurture to nature. Through the many hours of the series not one theologian was consulted. The not-so-subtle message of the program was that the Christian faith has nothing to add. It seems absurd that such a position can be held at all. The Christian faith on the contrary has a great deal to say concerning humanity. Much of this we have treated in the preceding chapters. Theology belongs in the discussion alongside psychology and sociology. The reverse of this also is true: Sociology and psychology have a valuable point of view for theology.

Part of what is implied by hearing the Scripture again is a vigorous proclamation of its truth. Christians have every right as citizens of the United States to participate fully in the political process. We do not have the right to mandate our beliefs on others, but we have a responsibility to offer our perspective. Jerry Falwell has helped the Church greatly by promoting the political power of Christians. Whether you agree or disagree with his positions is not important; he has done a great service to the Church. We can no doubt agree: "Churches need to become more active in the shaping of public policies having to do with sex."[10] No one else will proclaim the Christian point of view, therefore we must. This public policy is at the heart of a search for "the common dialogue."[11] One of the great advantages of being an American citizen is the right to influence public policy. It is, however, this broad access to government that can lead us to take it for granted. I am not advocating marching in picket lines or bombing abortion centers. My own preference is that we think through our faith by giving attention to the Scripture. After the process has gone on for a while, we should take the next step and express our viewpoint publicly.

The underlying assumption for all of this is the eternal truth of the Scripture. The relevance of the Scripture is that its message transforms lives. When we understand this, both a meaningful dialogue and the attempt to affect public policy will be possible. Neither is feasible until we search the Scriptures ourselves. Our forefathers did it, and we must do it as well. Hear the words of Paul addressed to Timothy: "Until I come, devote yourself to the public reading of Scripture, to preaching and to teaching. Do not neglect your gift, which was given you through a prophetic message . . . Watch your life and doctrine closely. Persevere in them, because if you do, you will save both yourself and your hearers" (1 Tim. 4:13-14, 16). This is still good advice.

4. **Reemphasize the importance of a Christian heritage.** According to Heb. 12:1 "we are surrounded by . . . a great cloud of witnesses." This verse is even more meaningful when we realize who these witnesses are: Abraham, Isaac, Jacob, Joseph, Moses, Gideon, and so on. The author is really asserting that as Christians, we enjoy the great blessing of a godly heritage. He could not have known those who would follow. People like Irenaeus, Augustine, Aquinas, Luther,

Wesley; and the list could go on. One of the clear messages taught by the Scriptures is that our heritage is important. It is important that we decide who we are and how we shall live.

Robert Bellah in his insightful book asserts the importance of "communities of memory."[12] These communities are places where people share a common history, thus a sense of what the world is all about. Bloom makes an important point:

> My grandparents were ignorant people by our standards, and my grandfather held only lowly jobs. But their home was spiritually rich because all the things done in it, not only what was specifically ritual, found their origin in the Bible's commandments, and their explanation in the Bible's stories and the commentaries on them, and had their imaginative counterparts in the deeds of the myriad of exemplary heroes.[13]

He goes on to add, "I do not believe that my generation, my cousins who have been educated in the American way, all of whom are M.D.s or Ph.D.s, have any comparable learning."[14] His point is well taken: We have lost any consensus in American life about reality. We no longer can agree on what is important. Sadly, this situation is beginning to characterize the church. It is not necessary to agree on every detail, but we no longer seem to be looking at the same landscape. Part of the answer would seem to be a vigorous attempt to reeducate ourselves concerning the biblical heroes, the Christian tradition. Who was Abraham and what did he do? Who was Wesley and why is he important? The loss of any understanding of these heroes is significant.

Being a Christian means that we understand or at least attempt to understand our tradition. It is possible that we have "raised a generation of kids who were robbed of their history and without inheritance."[15] The sense of place, of history must be consciously woven into everything we do. This kind of foundation will enable the Christian to be in community. In fact, "God has called us to come out of ourselves and to be 'in Christ.' To be in Christ means to be members of one another."[16] Therefore, an appreciation for heritage includes not only a sense of history but also a sense of community. We must for the most part dispense with the "lonely warrior" brand of Christianity. We are not alone, so let us live in conscious appreciation of community: "We have seen that however much Americans extol the autonomy and self-reliance of the individual, they do not imagine that a good life can be lived alone."[17]

An appreciation for our Christian heritage will help us avoid extreme individualism. We are in some respects at the very end of the "me generation." The self-indulgence that this slogan implies has carried with it stiff penalties. The church has not been immune:

"It is just You and me, God!"

"Since I am my own priest, who needs church?"

"Why not just worship God on the lake?"

"Everybody is equally right, as long as they believe it intensely."

People have made each of these statements to me from time to time. They illustrate the way private belief has replaced corporate responsibility. This extreme individualism is wrong in the light of Christian heritage. It leads to a sinful separation from one another. The New Testament is full of examples of corporate faith, of the strong sense in which people are responsible. Paul often refers to the brothers. The specific instructions of Paul to his churches also indicates the communal nature of New Testament faith.

According to Bellah, "The great contribution that the church idea can make today is its emphasis on the fact that individuality and society are not opposites but require each other."[18] Since we are not alone, it is important we "find" one another. We must seek to build a community of faith that reflects our commitment to one another. Never has it been more important than now to find community. We will not survive alone.

Recently I talked with a person at an altar of prayer. He had been a Christian but had fallen away. During this time he learned he had AIDS. The news drove him back to the church. Yet he had found no real peace. After several minutes of talking, it became evident that he was trying to cope with his problems all alone. He was failing. God calls us into community so that together we might walk with Him.

No doubt many other lessons will be learned from the cultural and intellectual currents surrounding the sexual revolution. We should not despair but rather find courage in the promise that God will sustain the Church. The excesses of the sexual revolution have been chronicled. The positive message has been emphasized. Together these should teach us to celebrate sexuality as God intended. The many pressures should remind us of the importance of the absolute. It should also drive us again into the Scripture, where we will find the eternal message of God. Finally, the sexual revolution should push us to reemphasize the importance of a Christian heritage.

We've examined many aspects of sexuality in this book. Some of the theology has been abstract, but untangling the sexual revolution will be more than an intellectual exercise. Theology is useful as it incarnates the gospel. This was certainly the case for Beth, a young woman who had lived a sexually indulgent life. Even though she bore the scars of her years of promiscuity, Beth was still a beautiful woman. One day God got ahold of her and changed everything. Several weeks later she stood in front of the church and said, "It feels good to be clean." Beth's story is the underlying message of this book. Beyond all of the theology, untangling the sexual revolution is the simple affirmation on the faces of people like Beth: "It feels good to be clean."

## Summary

1. The sexual revolution teaches us several important lessons.

2. A positive view of sexuality is central to the Christian faith.

3. We need to recover a healthy sense of the absolute.

4. The Scripture needs to be confronted again in our generation so that we might hear its message anew.

5. The Christian heritage needs to be reemphasized.

# Notes

1. Lane Dennis, "A Call to Holistic Salvation," in *The Orthodox Evangelicals,* ed. Robert Webber and Donald Bloesch (Nashville: Thomas Nelson Publishers, 1978), 97.

2. Nelson, "Reuniting Sexuality and Spirituality," 189.

3. Moore, "Teen-age Sexuality," 749.

4. Nancy Barcus, *Developing a Christian Mind* (Downers Grove, Ill.: InterVarsity Press, 1977), 19.

5. Paul Tillich, *Theology and Culture,* ed. Robert C. Kimball (New York: Oxford University Press, 1959), 301.

6. Ibid., 50.

7. Barcus, *Developing,* 11.

8. Richard Shaull, "Revolutionary Change in Theological Perspective," in *Social Ethics,* 252.

9. David Mace, *The Christian Response to the Sexual Revolution* (Nashville: Abingdon Press, 1970), 96.

10. Moore, "Teen-age Sexuality," 750.

11. Bellah, *Habits,* 307.

12. Ibid., 153.

13. Bloom, *Closing,* 60.

14. Ibid.

15. Sweet, "The 1960s," 42.

16. Edward Dayton, *Whatever Happened to Commitment?* (Grand Rapids: Zondervan Publishing House, 1984), 215.

17. Bellah, *Habits,* 84.

18. Ibid., 246-47.

# Suggestions for Further Reading*

Bellah, Robert, et al. *Habits of the Heart: Individualism and Commitment in American Life.* New York: Harper and Row, Publishers, 1985.

Bloom, Allan. *The Closing of the American Mind: How Higher Education Has Failed Democracy and Impoverished the Souls of Today's Students.* New York: Simon and Schuster, 1987.

Cahill, Lisa Sowle. *Between the Sexes: Foundations for a Christian Ethics of Sexuality.* Philadelphia: Fortress Press, 1985.

Dayton, Donald. *Discovering an Evangelical Heritage.* New York: Harper and Row, Publishers, 1976.

Frank, Douglas. *Less than Conquerors: How Evangelicals Entered the Twentieth Century.* Grand Rapids: William B. Eerdmans Publishing Co., 1986.

Jewett, Paul K. *Man as Male and Female: A Study in Sexual Relationships for a Theological Point of View.* Grand Rapids: William B. Eerdmans Publishing Co., 1975.

Mace, David. *The Christian Response to the Sexual Revolution.* Nashville: Abingdon Press, 1970.

Marsden, George, ed. *Evangelicalism and Modern America.* Grand Rapids: William B. Eerdmans Publishing Co., 1984.

Mollenkott, Virginia Ramey. *Women, Men, and the Bible* Nashville: Abingdon Press, 1977.

Nelson, James B. *Embodiment: An Approach to Sexuality and Christian Theology.* Minneapolis: Augsburg Publishing House, 1978.

Pittenger, W. Norman. *The Christian View of Sexual Behavior: A Reaction to the Kinsey Report.* Greenwich, Conn.: Seabury Press, 1954.

Ruether, Rosemary Radford. *New Woman—New Earth: Sexist Ideologies and Human Liberation.* New York: Seabury Press, 1975.

Smedes, Lewis B. *Sex for Christians: The Limits and Liberties of Sexual Living.* Grand Rapids: William B. Eerdmans Publishing Co., 1976.

*Please note that the author does not endorse all the positions represented by these books. These suggestions are offered to the person who would like to examine the issues raised in this book in more detail.